NEHEMIAH

a heart that can break

kelly minter

LifeWay Press®
Nashville, Tennessee

AUTHOR:

Kelly Minter

EDITORIAL PROJECT LEADER:

Amy Lowe

ART DIRECTOR & DESIGNER:

Christi Kearney

CONTENT EDITOR:

Dale McCleskey

PRODUCTION EDITOR:

Kailey Black

EXECUTIVE PRODUCER:

William H. Cox

VIDEO DIRECTOR:

April Dace

PHOTOGRAPHER & VIDEO EDITOR:

Julee Duwe

**SELECT INSTRUMENTAL
TRACKS FOR INTERVIEWS:**

Andrew Greer

**DVD INTRO SONG
"HEART OF MY GOD" WRITERS:**

Sarah Hart & Kelly Minter

Published by LifeWay Press®
© 2012 Kelly Minter
Second printing 2012

ISBN 978-1-4158-7342-7
Item 005371581

Dewey decimal classification: 259
Subject headings: COMPASSION \ BIBLE. O.T. NEHEMIAH \ MINISTRY

To order additional copies of this resource, write to LifeWay Church Resources Customer Service; One LifeWay Plaza; Nashville, TN 37234-0113; fax (615) 251-5933; phone (800) 458-2772; e-mail orderentry@lifeway.com; order online at www.lifeway.com; or visit the LifeWay Christian Store serving you.

Printed in the United States of America

Leadership and Adult Publishing
LifeWay Church Resources
One LifeWay Plaza
Nashville, TN 37234-0175

TABLE OF CONTENTS

MEET THE AUTHOR
KELLY MINTER

KELLY MINTER IS AN AUTHOR, SPEAKER, SONGWRITER, AND SINGER. SHE IS PASSIONATE ABOUT WOMEN DISCOVERING CHRIST THROUGH THE PAGES OF SCRIPTURE. SO WHETHER IT'S THROUGH A SONG, BIBLE STUDY, OR SPOKEN WORD, KELLY'S DESIRE IS TO AUTHENTICALLY EXPRESS CHRIST TO THE WOMEN OF THIS GENERATION. IN A CULTURE WHERE SO MANY ARE HURTING AND BROKEN, SHE LOVES TO SHARE ABOUT THE HEALING AND STRENGTH OF CHRIST THROUGH THE BIBLE'S TRUTH.

Her first Bible study, *No Other Gods,* which helps women unveil the false gods in their lives for the ultimate purpose of discovering freedom in the one, true God, is the first installment of *The Living Room Series. Ruth: Loss, Love & Legacy* focuses on the inspiring story of Ruth presented in the same *Living Room Series* format (studies can be done in any order).

Kelly writes extensively and speaks and leads worship at women's conferences, retreats, and events. She recorded *Loss, Love & Legacy* to complement *Ruth.* She also has a worship record entitled *Finer Day.* To view more of Kelly's music projects, books, studies, and calendar, visit *www.kellyminter.com.*

INTRODUCTION

WHEN SUMMER DESCENDS ON THE SOUTH, ITS HEAT AND HUMIDITY SCOOP US UP LIKE A BURLAP SACK THAT CINCHES ITS TIES AROUND US TILL ABOUT MID-SEPTEMBER. SOUTHERN SUMMERS DO THEIR BEST TO MAKE SURE NO ONE DOES WILD AND CRAZY THINGS LIKE BREATHE OR STRAIGHTEN ONE'S HAIR.

Of course there is always room for a brisk summer miracle like the one I experienced in a friend's backyard where a few of us grilled filets and vegetables we'd purchased earlier that morning from the Farmers' Market. Every Saturday we make an almost ceremonious trip there to pick up glass bottles of non-homogenized milk, meander through the mounds of local produce, zigzagging our way to Ray, a local farmer who sells the best free-range brown eggs, grass-fed beef, and chickens he'll proudly tell you live mostly off of ticks and bugs, as opposed to all that filler-based feed. I'm always relieved when I hear this because what could possibly be more appetizing than a chicken that regularly dines on ticks?

As the unruly orchestra of insects and birds serenaded us that evening, I was thankful for the peace and fullness God had restored to my life after years of hardship. The trouble was that despite all these blessings, I was battling a mounting discontentment: I was that odd blend of utterly thankful while feeling as if a significant piece was missing from the scene that, if found, would give this remarkable landscape its fuller and truer meaning. This is where Nehemiah comes in. Actually it's where ex-prisoners, Amazonians, an Indian tribe, Iraqi refugees, and a Brazilian woman named Clarinia who has cerebral palsy come in. Though I'd yet to meet any of them, I was missing them terribly. Let me explain …

As God is forming me into a more whole and free woman, I've begun to realize that freedom and healing aren't just so I can have exquisite friends, dwell in a peaceful home, attend an amazing church, make a comfortable salary, and eat tick-fed chicken. These are sublime blessings, but Christ has made us whole for far more than our own earthly comforts and pleasures. Essentially, wholeness is not the end but the very beginning, because wholeness allows us to give much more of our hearts, possessions, time, wisdom, money, friendship, and love away—a part of my Christianity that had been lacking.

As I sat in the unseasonable coolness of my friend's backyard—in the middle of all I'd ever hoped for—I told the Lord I was ready for more. Not that what He'd given me wasn't enough but that I wanted to use what He'd given me more intently for Him and His creation. Since that night I've befriended and taught women who'd just been released from prison. I've traveled several times to the Amazon where I encountered a tribe who had not a palm of shelter for their heads but whose countenances beamed with Christ. I have sung over Clarinia while my family rocked her back and forth in her hammock, a stretch of cloth she has laid in all her life. I've shared meals with an Iraqi family who'd fled Baghdad and have worked with my church in the aftermath of a devastating flood, meeting men and women who have seasoned my life in places I didn't know were so bland. And I was led to Nehemiah, a life-altering story of a man whose heart did not bow to earthly pleasures but instead broke for the suffering and vulnerable.

I write this to you with utmost humility because in all these relationships, I have been the chief recipient of the blessings. I can also honestly tell you that I daily battle selfishness and attachments to layers of earthly comforts; I am very much in process and have nothing close to a perfect equation for how much to give to those who have nothing to eat in proportion to how much to spend on a new piece of furniture. But then again, the command to love God and love others isn't a science project. It's a command that's intertwined with God transforming us into His own image and of us surrendering our lives back to Him.

Perhaps you are wondering what any of this has to do with the Book of Nehemiah, or how an others-centered curriculum relates to personal Bible study. My hope is that these answers will become clear over the next several pages as we study from Scripture God's call on each of our lives. As we discover a man whose heart broke for his people, so much so that he walked away from wealth, lavish comforts, and a prestigious position to reach his suffering brothers and sisters by helping rebuild the wall of their vitally important city.

Today I invite you to follow God outside of yourself. To consider the needs that surround you, and to listen closely to what breaks your heart. Because a broken heart is often the very thing God uses to restore the broken.

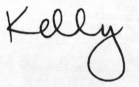

P.S. I want to thank my home group, who I call the "nogs" (Alli, Lauri, Carrie, and Anadara) for walking alongside me as I wrote Nehemiah. You will see many of their responses included throughout this study.

Gloria, director of Ray of Hope in Brazil
(See her ministry on session 1 video.)

SESSION 1
WHAT MAKES YOU WEEP?

I WAS SOMEWHERE IN THE AMAZON RAINFOREST WHEN OUR JUNGLE GUIDE MILTON STRUCK HIS MACHETE AGAINST THE THICK TRUNK OF AN INNOCENT TREE, CAUSING IT TO BLEED A MILKY LIQUID ONLY HE COULD HAVE ANTICIPATED. LIKE A SAGE DETECTIVE MILTON KNEW WHAT HE WAS LOOKING FOR, A PARTICULAR TREE THAT PRODUCES A WHITE MEDICINAL SUBSTANCE THAT SETTLES UPSET STOMACHS. THIS WAS GOOD TO KNOW IN THE EVENT I EVER MISPLACED MY TUMS IN THE JUNGLE—I COULD NOW FALL BACK ON THIS TREE AND A MACHETE, WHICH I FOUND MINIMALLY COMFORTING.

A few steps beyond the medicine tree Milton spotted what looked like a gargantuan coconut shell. But lest you think about cracking one of these open, let me save you the trouble by letting you know it was home to approximately 42 zillion ants. Our other jungle guide Tiago tapped on this "coconut," a minor disturbance in our minds but for these miniature creatures, the equivalent of a 7.2 earthquake on the ant Richter scale. Like candy falling from a pinata, tiny ants rained all over his body. Wasting no time he smothered them onto his head, face, and arms, as if he were lathering on sunscreen. He explained that this created a natural insect repellent while neutralizing his body's scent, which is a good idea when hunting. You'd hate to have one of those panthers sniff you out— the one that woke up thinking how good a Tiago wrap would be for lunch.

Beyond the heap of ants was the impressive walking tree. As other trees around it cast their shade, the walking tree grows new roots or "legs" on the side in the direction of the sunlight. Meanwhile the legs left in the shade dry up, thus it walks around. Before you get too excited, this is not the kind of tree you'd ask to be your walking buddy because it only moves a few feet a year, and this pace has not been scientifically proven to burn calories. But give it time—the "Walking Tree Diet" could eventually catch on.

Past the walking tree we saw animal prints, bugs brand new to my eye, florescent birds, nuts, you name it. In fact, the Amazon is the place where I held my first unprocessed cashew nut. I know now why they cost so much—why when the outside packaging boasts of mixed nuts, the container's inventory is made up of approximately 87 percent peanuts, 6 percent walnuts, 5 percent Brazilian nuts, and two cashews that are the first to go like the prize out of a Cracker Jacks box. While still on the tree, the cashew is attached to a pear-sized fruit and is technically a seed encased in a hard shell that is toxic and will make your mouth break out in sores. See, this is why God stuffed the cashew with so many calories and then stored it in a sheath of poison, so we would pace ourselves.

After a few mouth blisters you may decide you're only in the mood for one cashew, which is a good thing because more than three will make you fat. Then of course we, in all our brilliance, came up with processing machines and roasting techniques that now allow us to bypass the toxic shell as we reach into a tin can and pop cashews at 9 calories apiece, doing nothing but having cracked a lid. Ah, the genius of westernization.

Each time I visit the Amazon, I explore whatever our jungle guides point out to us, knowing full well we are only scratching the surface of the treasure the rainforest has to offer. As we work our way through a book like Nehemiah we will similarly see wondrous things, but we won't see it all. As Milton and Tiago highlighted what we needed to know about the Amazon, so I will tug on the threads in Nehemiah I find especially significant. My goal is not to uncover every word but to follow missional themes about service, kingdom work, tender hearts, prayer, love of the poor, the sacredness of Scripture, and others God has been stirring in my heart over the past few years. These themes run straight into our daily commission as New Testament believers.

WHILE STANDING WITH MY CASHEW ON THE EDGE OF A PRECIPICE OVERLOOKING THE RIO NEGRO, I HAD A MOMENT WITH GOD IN THE MIDST OF HIS CREATION.

In our processed, technologically spun world sometimes we can get so far removed from the origin of things—and this goes for even our spiritual diets. As we spend focused time with the Lord in the Book of Nehemiah, my prayer is that we will hear His voice and see His path for our lives with finer clarity. I know we all have more to do than we can fit in daylight's hours, but try not to rush. Sit with Him long enough for the treasures of His Word to emerge like rainforest creatures sneaking out of their protective logs or leaping from their nests in plain enough view for you to be in awe of their splendor. I would tell you to grab your machete and a handful of ants, but I am thinking your Bible and a pen will do. So many surprises are waiting.

VIDEO 1

The time line
Kelly references
is on page 13.

NOTES:

_____

_____

_____

_____

_____

_____

_____

_____

_____

_____

_____

How does Nehemiah's compassionate heart stir your own heart to love and service?

How did it affect you to learn that Nehemiah heard about the Jews' suffering while living in a Persian Resort?

What about Gloria's interview struck you the most? How did she inspire, challenge, encourage you?

Video sessions are available for download at *www.lifeway.com/women*

DAY 01

A HEART THAT CAN BREAK

Whenever we begin studying a new book of the Bible, especially an historical one like Nehemiah, we need to get an understanding of the landscape. What was the cultural climate? What was going on in the world at the time? Were the people at war or at peace? How did they like their eggs? As we settle into the Book of Nehemiah we'll consider the setting of Jerusalem and the history of the Jews, making our journey through this book all the more meaningful. Read Nehemiah 1:1-4.

A Sketch of Jerusalem: To understand the significance of Jerusalem's broken-down walls, we must know the significance of Jerusalem itself. The first mention of Jerusalem (Salem) appears in Genesis 14:17-20 where we meet Melchizedek, the priest of Salem. Approximately 30 years later, God told Abraham to offer his son Isaac as an offering on Mount Moriah (see Gen. 22). Abraham's offering foreshadowed what would one day happen on the same mountain, where God would offer up His own Son, Jesus Christ. Several hundred years after Abraham's offering, King David conquered Jerusalem, driving out the Jebusites. Already, we can see the significance of Jerusalem mounting.

> Read 1 Chronicles 11:4-9. What two other names did King David give Jerusalem in verses 5 and 7? "Z_____" and "the _____ of _____"

In 1 Chronicles 15:1-16, David brought the ark of God into Jerusalem. Since the ark represented the place of God's dwelling, this event marked another significant milestone in Jerusalem's history. After bringing the ark to Jerusalem, David had a heart to build a more permanent dwelling place for the Name of the Lord (see 1 Chron. 22:6-10).

Though David's desire pleased God, it was His will that David's son Solomon be the one to build the temple. After Solomon's death, Israel was divided into two parts: Israel became the Northern part of the Kingdom and Judah became the Southern Kingdom—Jerusalem was the capitol city of Judah. A succession of 20 kings ruled Judah from 979–586 B.C., many of whom were evil and disobedient. In 586 B.C. the Babylonian king Nebuchadnezzar conquered Jerusalem and forever marred its history.

> Read 2 Chronicles 36:15-23. What did Nebuchadnezzar do to the city of Jerusalem?

What did he do with the people living there?

The people lived in exile until what other kingdom came into power (see v. 20)?

Approximately 70 years after the Jews were carried into captivity, King Cyrus of Persia conquered Babylon. He granted the Jews freedom to return to their homeland and rebuild their temple (see Ezra 2:1). Approximately 71 years after the exiles returned, Nehemiah heard of Jerusalem's tragic condition. This brings us up to where we left off in Nehemiah 1:1-4. See the time line in the margin.

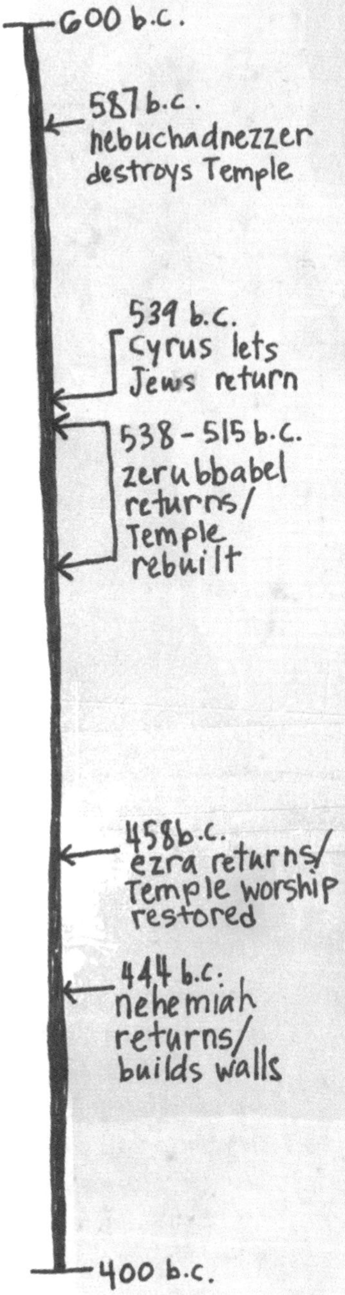

So many fascinating elements reside in God's authoring of Jerusalem, and He's still writing its story. It's a story that covers not only a physical Jerusalem but also the Jerusalem from above. We'll look more closely at this in days to come, but for now take another look at Nehemiah 1:1-2.

> **How did Nehemiah learn the condition of Jerusalem?**
> ○ He received a letter from Jerusalem's king.
> ○ He asked his visiting brother Hanani.
> ○ A messenger delivered the information.

We're not even two verses in, and I'm immediately hit with a distinctive quality about Nehemiah: He wanted to know. Sometimes I shield myself from finding out what's really going on with people for fear I'll be held responsible. Because with information often comes responsibility; if we know, we might be required to *do* something.

We'll get to this later, but note that Nehemiah was a Jew, born in Persia during the exile, meaning he had relatives in Jerusalem. Though the suffering of the Jews would have naturally been of some concern to him, technically this was not his problem. He didn't live there.

> **Reread Nehemiah 1:3-4. What did Nehemiah do in response to the news about Jerusalem?**

PERSONAL TAKE: What does his response tell you about his heart?

Timeline (margin):

600 b.c.

587 b.c.
nebuchadnezzer destroys Temple

539 b.c.
Cyrus lets Jews return

538 – 515 b.c.
zerubbabel returns/ Temple rebuilt

458 b.c.
ezra returns/ Temple worship restored

444 b.c:
nehemiah returns/ builds walls

400 b.c.

Nehemiah had to have a heart that could break to restore a wall that was broken. Over the years many have pegged Nehemiah as a phenomenally skilled leader because of what he accomplished in Jerusalem. I agree with this assessment, but sometimes I wonder if Nehemiah was a great leader because of his skills or because he had a God-inspired heart that couldn't bear the thought of letting his fellow Jews suffer—a heart that had no choice but to *do something!*

Many naturally gifted leaders exist, but those who lead out of a sheer necessity have a zeal that can't be quenched. So often we exalt the most skilled, the strongest leaders, the deeply resourced and connected. But we can't underestimate the power that pours forth from a broken heart. Think of what has been accomplished over the years by ordinary people simply because they were moved over the hurting, the poor, the outsider, the sick. Think of the world-impacting organizations that have been started by leaders with little education, mediocre communication skills, or zero dollars. Sometimes the most accomplished people aren't the ones with the most ability but with the most breakable hearts.

///

GROUP DISCUSSION:
Write your thoughts about one of the following:

1. Describe a time when you didn't want to know something because you didn't want to be responsible to carry another burden.

2. Describe a time when you opened yourself up to the struggle of someone else and how this affected you.

What breaks your heart?	Where could you be more tender?

I wrote in my journal, "Perhaps many could have done the work of Nehemiah, but his heart was tender enough to break. Maybe no one else cared that much." Most of us have hearts that can break for matters personally affecting us, but how many of our hearts break over the suffering of others? If I see anything in today's study, it's that Nehemiah had a heart that could break for others. End today by praying that God will give you compassion in the areas where your heart may be a little cold or numb, that He would develop in you the heart Jesus has for others. It's what I'm praying for myself. Lord, keep breaking our hearts!

DAY 02
THE FIRST PLACE YOU TURN

A couple of years ago I started praying one morning a week with some of my dearest friends because I figured that doing prayer is probably the best way to get better at it. Since I've never found prayer to be the easiest or most natural part of my Christian life, I love when I get the chance to be around a true pray-ER.

I talked with one of these enviable souls while strolling the English city of Lewis on a break from a worship conference where I was speaking. Karin is now my dear friend from Sweden, but at the time I was just getting to know her as we walked the steep roads of Lewis. I'll never forget when Karin casually mentioned that she prays for an hour every morning as part of her regular routine.

"Oh yeah, me too" was what I wanted to come tumbling out of my mouth as I cradled my latte, except this would have been what the Brits call a falsehood. Since that afternoon, I've asked Karin a lot of questions about prayer while spending time praying with her, because I'm really moved by this kind of intimacy with Jesus.

If the thought of an hour of prayer a day makes you cave with guilt, the idea is not to seek a magical time frame but the fellowship, closeness, and power that comes along with an ever-deeper prayer life. For the next two days we're going to study Nehemiah's prayer as recorded in 1:5-11. These verses serve as a summary of the substance of the prayers he prayed "day and night" (v. 6) for several months. They express the content and themes of his petitions, which often drew from passages in Deuteronomy that had become well-known liturgical prayers of his day. Still, Nehemiah interspersed personal pleas that are not found elsewhere, so we see that while he leaned on Israel's liturgical traditions, he was free to petition God about his specific circumstances.[1]

Ask the Holy Spirit to reveal His Word to you today and read Nehemiah 1:5-11. Write anything that stands out to you.

Oswald Chambers has been credited with saying, "Too often we treat prayer as the preparation for the work of the church. Do you not see? Prayer _is_ the work of the church."[2]

If we can absorb this quote into our thinking it will radically change the way we view prayer. Notice that when Nehemiah heard about Jerusalem's tragic state he didn't call a meeting, gather his smartest friends together for a think tank, or take a poll about what should be done. Though these may have been valuable options for later, the first thing he did was pray. I think he knew that prayer was just as much a part of the work as any physical action he might one day take. ✚

Is your knee-jerk reaction to cry out to the One who is all-powerful, who is merciful, and who deeply loves you? Or do you turn to your own resources, closest friends, most powerful relationships? Do you shy away from prayer because of a lack of trust or intimacy with God? Do you feel safer keeping things in your own hands and under your own control? Take time to consider these areas of unbelief, and ask God to work out in you a greater trust in Him.

+

PERSONAL REFLECTION:
When faced with a difficult situation, to whom or what do you normally turn first?

When you look closely at Nehemiah's prayer, it's clear he gained his reference point from Scripture. I find this reliance on God's Word impactful because it shows how valuable a working knowledge of the Bible is to our prayers. Nehemiah petitioned God based on what had been revealed about Him in the Old Testament. We are free to do the same—only with a much bigger Bible from which to pull.

PERSONAL TAKE : **In what ways does your knowledge of the Bible play a part in your prayers? How can you strengthen this?**

///

GROUP DISCUSSION:
What gets in the way of your turning to God first? Feel free to discuss external as well as internal obstacles, such as lack of trust, fear, lack of intimacy, and so forth.

For the rest of today's study, we'll focus on the names and attributes by which Nehemiah addressed God, reminding us that the way we approach Him is as important as what we ask of Him.

Nehemiah opened his prayer with the divine name:
○ Lᴏʀᴅ (Yahweh)   ○ Jesus
○ Father   ○ El Roi

When you see Lᴏʀᴅ in all caps, it's the personal name God gave Himself in relation to His chosen people Israel, a name based on love and familiarity. It's the name Yahweh.

GOD OF HEAVEN : After Nehemiah opened his prayer with this personal name, he then addressed Him as the "God of heaven" (v. 5). The distinction of our Father reigning in heaven versus only on earth may seem obvious, but we must remind ourselves that we do not serve a human king with feet of clay, bound by the limitations of flesh and sin. He lives outside of time, beyond our limited strength, and holds all things in His hands. Yes, He invites us to invoke Him on a personal level as Yahweh, but simultaneously He remains the God of all heaven. Think of Jesus's words in Matthew 6:10, "Your will be done on earth as it is in heaven."

GREAT AND AWESOME GOD : Nehemiah attributed the word "awesome" to the Lord (1:5, NIV). The Holman Christian Standard Bible translates it as "awe-inspiring."

In the margin describe the last time you were awestruck by God.

I'll be the first to admit that I long to be *awestruck* in God's presence more than I am. I believe my lack of awestruck moments isn't because God is lacking in awesomeness but because I settle for so much less. I'm willing for my worship experience to be mediocre as long as I'm eating at a fabulous restaurant with friends after church. I'll settle for far less than awestruck in my prayer time, assuming I've got other forms of community planned for the day. When our bills are being paid, our children are behaving, we've got multiple outlets of fun to plug into, and life is generally fulfilling, do we really need something as dramatic as awestruck? This can often be the mentality, but being entertained by earthly pleasures cannot compare to being awed in God's presence. My prayer is that you and I won't settle for substitutes, because we all need to be regularly astounded by His majesty if we are to truly know Him and testify to others about who He is.

The following verses have this same word *awesome* in them. Identify what God's awesomeness is attached to in each.

Genesis 28:16-17

Exodus 15:11

Psalm 65:5

Psalm 99:3

HESED: Consider one more aspect of Nehemiah's prayer in 1:5.

Fill in the blanks: "O LORD, God of heaven, the great and awesome God, who keeps his _____ of _____ with those who love him and obey his commands" (NIV).

Bible translations differ slightly here, but the Hebrew word for God's covenant of love is *hesed,* which means, "unfailing love, loyal love, devotion, kindness, often based on a prior relationship, especially a *covenant relationship*" (emphasis added).[3] The word hesed is often translated in our Bibles as "love" or "kindness" because we don't have an English word that accurately expresses it. One of the best ways to understand the meaning of hesed is to pull out a concordance and look up its usages in various places. After seeing it used in different lights, your understanding of its meaning will begin to take shape. Read the verses below, noting that anytime you see the word "love" in the following passages, the translation is hesed.

THROUGH LOVE AND FAITHFULNESS SIN IS ATONED FOR; THROUGH THE FEAR OF THE LORD A MAN AVOIDS EVIL.

PROVERBS 16:6, NIV

Read Psalm 31:21-22. According to the psalmist, in what kinds of circumstances can we experience God's hesed?

What tangible benefits of God's hesed appear in Psalm 40:11; 119:76?

True / False: Hesed atones for sin (see Prov. 16:6 in margin).

According to Isaiah 54:10, hesed is:
○ conditional   ○ predictable
○ unshakable   ○ fickle

You may have wondered, *if God's* hesed *is so unconditional and free why does He keep it "with those who love Him and keep His commands?"* (Neh. 1:5). The idea is not that God's hesed for us is conditional but that His love compels us to love Him back with affection and obedience. It's a gracious circle that begins and ends with God, enabling us to love Him in return, a love that doesn't allow us to live cheaply but fully! A bit of a mystery perhaps, but one worth embracing.

Write below the four highlighted names and attributes of God we discussed today. I'll fill in the first one:

1. LORD (Yahweh)
2.
3.
4.

PERSONAL REFLECTION: In closing, which of these four is the most meaningful to you right now, and why? After recording your thoughts end with a prayer of thanksgiving.

DAY 03

THE WONDER OF PRAYER

During the cold and dreary month of January, after all the celebrations had ceased and nothing remained to look forward to but credit card bills from Christmas and a looming quarterly tax payment, I escaped to the Amazon. (I've determined this to be the one place on earth where bills have trouble finding you.) In addition to fleeing from responsibility, I was there to interview 25 jungle pastors. After listening to each of their stories I have volumes of musings I could release unfettered onto the page, but instead I will leave you with the one truth I walked away with: **WE WILL ACCOMPLISH LITTLE OF ETERNAL SIGNIFICANCE APART FROM PRAYER.**

I interviewed pastor after pastor and the one recurring theme I heard was that God moves in response to prayer. The impact of their stories called forth life in areas of my soul that had long since stopped believing on the level they believe. Their faith in God, and therefore in prayer, is exceedingly deep because they have nothing else, no other options, no resources to fall back on. Jesus is truly their all-in-all, a reliance I know but not to the degree they know it. They bear witness to astounding answers to prayer that many of us never see because they need Him for all of life. This is not to make us feel bad about the societies we live in but to remind us that God has called us to seek Him first and with everything we have. So it is too fitting that today we will read the rest of Nehemiah's prayer, a prayer I can never look at the same again. Read Nehemiah 1:6-7.

Whose sins did Nehemiah confess?

In what ways had he/they acted?
- ○ tolerably
- ○ permissibly
- ○ mistakenly
- ○ corruptly

What had the people failed to do?

Generally speaking we refer to very little as "sin" anymore, much less evil or wicked. Our culture doesn't place much emphasis on these ideas, primarily because we have rejected the absolutes of right and wrong, good and bad, moral and immoral. As a rule, we don't want to be hemmed in by rigid constraints, instead embracing the idea that we're all basically good people and should be left alone to define our morality. But we can never leave the job of defining sin to any person or culture. Only the Lord has this right. He is the One who determines what sin is and reveals its gravity. If we view our sin as a minor infringement we will view God's forgiveness with equal mediocrity. We can't appreciate the great cost of forgiveness if we think our sin barely needed it in the first place.

I appreciate Nehemiah's humility in identifying with the sin of Israel. He knew that the demise of Jerusalem was because God's people had turned against Him, and even though he wasn't personally living in the middle of it, he was aware that he too needed pardoning. If you're anything like me, you have a tendency to measure everyone else's "bigger" sin against your far lesser, more tolerable mistakes. When we do this we set ourselves up for believing that other people need God's grace and forgiveness much more than we do. This is to fail to see our sin. Notice this was not Nehemiah's approach.

III

GROUP DISCUSSION: What role does repentance play in your prayer life? If very little, why do you think this is so? If it's an important part of your prayers, discuss its benefits.

What surprising characteristic of God leads us to repentance according to Romans 2:4?

We may be conditioned to think that God's wrath or judgment leads us to repentance, but how amazing is it that it is His kindness? A kindness that brings us to the place where we literally "turn around." So if you're unsure of where to start in the process of repentance, ask God for His kindness to take you there. Look again at Nehemiah 1:8-10.

> **What had God promised to do if His people returned to Him and obeyed His commands? (Nehemiah is referencing an earlier quote from Deuteronomy where this promise was given through Moses.)**

Notice that Nehemiah prayed on behalf of his Jewish brothers and sisters, which is a special kind of prayer we often refer to as *intercessory prayer*. Certainly we are to seek God for personal wisdom, guidance, blessing, healing, and much more, but it's vital that we devote time praying for others. This is a part of my prayer life that God has been stretching me in, and, as my pastor's wife so eloquently reminds our congregation, this is not only our responsibility but also our exquisite honor. If I may add to that, one of the beauties of intercessory prayer is that it builds community as it divinely attaches you to those for whom you are praying.

One of my goals in this study is to connect the Book of Nehemiah to the much larger work of Scripture, giving you a fuller grasp of the themes that run throughout the Bible. Since intercessory prayer is one of them, take a look at the following New Testament passages that address the significance of intercessory prayer.

> **What did Paul consistently pray for the Ephesians in 1:15-18?**

> **What verb is used to describe Epaphras's prayer for the Colossians in 4:12-13?**

> **In 1 Thessalonians 1:2-3 did Paul plead for the Thessalonians or celebrate them in his prayer?**

Paul let the Thessalonians know that he'd rehearsed their faith-inspired works, labors of love, and hopeful endurance in the presence of God.

This is a unique concept because it's a thanks-based intercession, as opposed to a petition-based one. In a sense, Paul was reminding God of how awesome these believers were. ✚

Close out the first chapter of Nehemiah by reading verse 11. Who is the person Nehemiah refers to as "this man"?

What was Nehemiah's position?

The end of chapter 1 reveals the moment prior to Nehemiah finally taking action ("Give Your servant success today") and reveals to us a key individual, the king. Tomorrow we will explore this further, but in the meantime, let your heart and mind rest on the beauty and riches of prayer. Oh, that we may know the power and intimacy of prayer like the jungle pastors. Like Nehemiah. Like the godly men and women we remembered before God today. If you don't know where to start in prayer, follow the pattern of Nehemiah: praise God, thank Him for His covenant love, repeat His promises back to Him, remind Him of His ways, repent of what you have done and what you have left undone.

I hope that God is deepening your prayer life, as He has been mine. Prayer is a commitment that can't be based on feeling because we won't always feel it. Usually it's something we have to work at just like any other piece of our Christian life. I am encouraged by the simple words spoken by one of the disciples, "Lord, *teach us* to pray" (Luke 11:1, emphasis added). How I need to be taught, and how humbly these jungle pastors instructed me without even knowing it. I thought I had come there for them, but they were the ones who were there for me.

+
PERSONAL REFLECTION: Take a minute to thank God for an incredible person of faith in your life, rehearsing some of their loving acts of service.

PERSONAL RESPONSE: Write down a few people who need you to intercede for them. Be thoughtful about your list, writing down the names you can truly commit to praying for. Remind yourself to come back to this list several times throughout our study.

DAY 04
TO BE AFRAID

I would not say that evangelism is at the top of my spiritual-gifts list, if you consider evangelism a "gift." It's probably better characterized as a command which means less excuses for me like, "It's not how I'm wired." For the past several months, however, I've had a new urgency to share the gospel in a way I've never experienced before. So when my doctor scheduled me for three months of physical therapy, it became the natural setting for me to talk with my therapist about God. Well, natural may be a stretch—it became the place where I chose to speak about Jesus and set aside everything in me that desires to be accepted, appear normal, and generally not be thought of as a nutcase.

By the end of the three months I had shared a little about my own life and showed my genuine care for my new friend by bringing her back a pound of organic coffee from San Francisco. How does this say anything other than, "Jesus loves you"? But we hadn't gotten anywhere near the finer principles of the gospel, things like sin and the cross, and I was afraid I wouldn't see her again. Then the Lord began nudging me to call my therapist at her office and invite her to church, or something less threatening out of the gates, like lunch. It would be difficult for me to explain how uncomfortable I was with this idea, but dread may have been included. *Lord, please don't make me do something as awkward as call her office! Can you not just send an angel or something?*

I couldn't get rid of the nudging though—the Holy Spirit shines when it comes to relentlessness—so I picked up the phone. To my great surprise my therapist sounded delighted to get together and suggested we meet up for a walk. We ended up having an incredibly honest conversation about our beliefs about God, Jesus, the Bible, and the church. We talked about our upbringings, and though we shared very different perspectives, I couldn't think of a time in the past year when I'd felt so certain I was exactly where I was supposed to be doing exactly what I was supposed to do. It was a deeply energizing experience because I had done it all in faith and because God had given me a passion for this woman to know how much Jesus loves her.

I know you're wondering what in the entire universe this has to do with Nehemiah. Hopefully this will become clear as you read the first 10 verses of chapter 2. The question I want you to keep in mind is, "Of what are you afraid when it comes to the gospel?" For me, a simple phone call terrified me. Keep in mind that when I use the term "gospel," I don't only mean sharing the message of salvation with a person who doesn't know Jesus. I mean anything that goes along with leading gospel-inspired lives. In the margin write the first few fears that come to mind.

Now read Nehemiah 2:1-10. Of what was Nehemiah afraid?

For a little more background, read Ezra 4:8-23. Who had ordered a decree to stop the rebuilding of Jerusalem?

How does this information further explain Nehemiah's great fears in approaching King Artaxerxes with his particular request?

We discovered yesterday that Nehemiah was cupbearer to the king. This was a position of high honor in the royal household and was well regarded by the Persians. The cupbearer (or butler) was in charge of choosing the wine, tasting it to make sure it had not been poisoned, and then serving it to the king. This position gave Nehemiah regular access to King Artaxerxes and put him in a place of potential influence.

I find it interesting that Nehemiah's mention of being cupbearer to the king immediately followed his recorded prayer to *the* King. We may be tempted to think that if we've got the support of the most powerful person in our sphere we're set. Nehemiah knew this wasn't true. He knew he needed the King of the Universe more than the king of Persia. Before going any further, I want us to have a handle on the time frame between when Nehemiah first heard about the demise of Jerusalem and his meeting with King Artaxerxes.

With what month does chapter 2 begin?

With what month does chapter 1 begin?

The month of Chislev (Kislev) is equivalent to our late November to early December, and Nisan corresponds with our late March to early April.[4] This means that Nehemiah had been praying for four months, night and day, before finding himself in the position with the king we just read about. ✚

The passing of time speaks to Nehemiah's persistence in prayer and the discipline of waiting on the Lord for his moment of action. This is a convicting model for me because often I am more comfortable taking action than I am sitting quietly before the Lord, waiting and listening for His voice. My attitude is shifting as I increasingly experience the power of prayer. I am learning that God can accomplish far more than what my highest thoughts and most skillful actions can achieve. Not to mention the intimacy of knowing that I am being led by Him, as opposed to taking my best shot at things, hoping He will bless my aim.

When I look at the exchange between the king and Nehemiah, I see the prework of prayer all over the place. The flow of this conversation is a marvel, especially realizing that Artaxerxes was the one who had ordered the work to stop in Jerusalem.

I wonder if Nehemiah had asked God to make a way for him during his four months of prayer, because doors were flinging open in unlikely succession. By the end of these 10 verses he was getting everything he had requested and more. I would have taken this prime opportunity to additionally ask for a going-away party: *And may all the people bring me gift cards to my favorite furniture stores … Long live the king!*

PERSONAL TAKE: Do you think Nehemiah's sorrow of heart couldn't be contained, or do you think he purposely expressed his sadness in the king's presence?

Given Nehemiah's nerves, we can appreciate the king starting the conversation by asking what was wrong. This was the first door God blew open, paving the way for Nehemiah to explain by responding to

+

PERSONAL RESPONSE: How does this passage of time encourage you to keep praying for something you've been praying about for a long time?

///

GROUP DISCUSSION: Describe a time when you were dreading a conversation that turned out much better than you anticipated. Did prayer play a part in the outcome? How?

Artaxerxes' question. Still Nehemiah was extremely afraid to be honest. One misstep and it could cost him his job, even his life.

As readers we can feel Nehemiah's terror, anxious for the king to put him out of his misery by suggesting he go and help his countrymen. But Artaxerxes didn't do this right away. Instead, he wanted more clarity. Nehemiah was forced to state his case, which I imagine was his biggest fear. In the moment I don't usually love this about God, but after the fact I am always pleased that He didn't give me an easy way out. He often makes us do the thing—or say the thing. Nehemiah had to spell out his specific request to the king (and queen) and detail what it was he wanted to do. This was the hard part.

What did Nehemiah specifically ask Artaxerxes for in 2:5?

What did he immediately do before this (see v. 4)?

How did the king answer?
○ yes   ○ no   ○ neither

After further requesting letters of safe conduct and lumber from Asaph, the king threw in a military escort which promised further protection from neighboring governors. Nehemiah's encounter with Artaxerxes couldn't have gone any better, and although this was an enormous feat, his work was just beginning.

How did others react to Nehemiah's success (see v. 10)?

We'll have plenty of time to discuss Sanballat and Tobiah in the coming days because this is not even sort of the end of them, as "These two men will throw a long shadow over the story."[5] Putting them aside for the time being, I want to focus on one of the most meaningful phrases in the book.

Finish the sentence (NIV): "They were very much disturbed that someone had come to _____."

I hope you can allow this sentence to penetrate your heart. You may not be in a position to leave your job like Nehemiah, but surely there is someone whose well-being you can seek and promote. Perhaps it's someone living overseas in a country not as affluent as your own. It may be a family member. It may require the personal sacrifice of money, time, or emotional energy. It could mean praying for courage and asking someone to dinner, church, or a walk in the park. Perhaps there's a group of young women you can teach the Bible to, even if you don't think of yourself as a Bible teacher. When embraced by God's grace, the call to serve is no longer a guilt-trip but the gospel. ✚

Sometimes we make this more difficult than it is. When my sister Katie returned from one of our trips to the Amazon, she was struggling with how she could serve in her own community. With one phone call to her home church she was put in touch with two grown Lebanese sisters who are raising eight children together in the same home. Katie asked what their needs were and without hesitation they explained that they were having a hard time putting food on the table for all their children, despite working hard at minimum wage. Katie packed up her own two children, headed to the grocery store, and then delivered food and toys to their home. Next thing she knew she was picking up six of the eight children and carting them off to Vacation Bible School the next week. One of the little boys said that VBS had been the best week of his whole summer.

A Lebanese family who's never heard about God's love is hearing about Him today. Katie's family, who is desperately seeking their welfare, has been significantly blessed by these adorable children and hardworking mothers. They didn't have to cross the sea to meet them, only the street—and their fear of stepping beyond the familiar.

What has God put in your heart to do?

+

PERSONAL RESPONSE: Whose welfare are you promoting and how? If God is asking you for a commitment, write about whose well-being you will begin to seek.

DAY 05

WHAT HAS GOD PUT IN YOUR HEART?

Read Nehemiah 2:11-12 and fill in the blanks below.

"I didn't tell anyone what my _____ had laid on my _____ to do for Jerusalem."

Today we're going to focus our attention on this single sentence. I will use the one-phrase-only approach sparingly in our study for obvious reasons—I'd hate to still be in the Book of Nehemiah 37 years from now. But occasionally a verse like this requires more than a passing comment.

To me, this sentence is one of the most important in the book, because it shows God placed the desire to rebuild the walls of Jerusalem in Nehemiah's heart. This is so foundational because it sheds light on if and how God speaks to us. It shows how our passions intersect God's will for us. Is it possible that God still puts dreams in our hearts today, and are these dreams and desires legitimate lighthouses we are to follow? These are a few of the questions on which we will focus as we tie up our week.

Turn to 1 Chronicles 17:1-2. What did David have in his heart to do for God? (Some translations say "mind.")

How does this compare to what Nehemiah had in his heart to do?

Continue reading verses 17:3-4,11-14. Who was the one who would accomplish what David had in his heart to do?

How is this different from Nehemiah's project?

Turn over a few pages to 1 Chronicles 22:6-10. Why did God determine that David was not the one to build His temple?

Writing Bible studies and speaking at women's events had never visited my thoughts when I left Washington, D.C. for Music City at the whipper-snapperish age of 23. I had a heart to impact people with the love of Christ, and I had worked out how I was going to do this through what I had hoped to be a wildly successful music career. (Incidentally, I found the music industry to be one of God's most effective instruments when He's looking to humble someone.)

Though music will always be a part of what I do, my life and ministry have taken shape with curves and angles I had never envisioned. This may be why I so appreciate this passage about David's yearning to build a house for God, because things turned out so differently than he'd imagined. God still honored David's desire, and the house still got built. Just not by David but by his son Solomon.

The following verses span the opening lines of Solomon's prayer regarding the newly constructed temple in Jerusalem. Read 1 Kings 8:14-19. Pay special attention to verses 17-18 (NIV) below.

> **Circle the word "heart" every time it is mentioned in the passage below. Your translation may use the word "desire."**

> My father David had it in his heart to build a temple for the Name of the LORD, the God of Israel. But the LORD said to my father David, "Because it was in your heart to build a temple for my Name, you did well to have this in your heart."

PERSONAL TAKE: Describe the way you see the blending of God's hand building His house (see vv. 15-16) with the desire David had in his heart for this to be accomplished (see vv. 17-18). In other words, how are man and God seen mysteriously working together here?

///

GROUP DISCUSSION: Have you ever had a vision to do something for God that turned out differently than what you'd planned? Describe your desire and the way God led you in it.

I love the phrase, "You did well to have this in your heart" (v. 18. NIV). After many years of running from Saul, fighting tumultuous wars, and waiting for the day he would officially be crowned king, David finally settled into his cedar palace. He could have propped his feet up and taken a generous breath of kingdom air. He could have called for a massage or ordered up a cluster of grapes while admiring the jewels on his crown. But something was seriously askew; David was thriving under the cedar beams of his palace while the dwelling place of Almighty God lie under a tent. Indeed David *did well* to respond to this tension by desiring to build God a magnificent house, even if God came back with a different way to execute David's plan by entrusting the project to Solomon.

It's no coincidence that both David and Nehemiah were living or serving in palaces when an astonishing need tugged on their hearts. The royal decorum, fine wine, and comfortable existence at their disposal did not erase the reality that walls had been broken down in Jerusalem or that God's dwelling place was without a proper temple. May I suggest that we are living in equally disproportionate days. Though many of us do not have unlimited wealth or descend from royalty, most of us dwell in a far wealthier state than the rest of the world. This is not a truth meant to paralyze us beneath the weight of overwhelming guilt but an urgent call for us to stop and ask the Lord, "What have You put in my heart to do?"

I fear that while much of the Western church slumbers in its palace of comfort, many who desperately need our resources, both spiritual and material, are suffering greatly. Like David and Nehemiah, we must be willing to sacrifice our own comforts and protections for the sake of others. Here's the wonderful news: neither of these men dreaded the thought of making such sacrifices. Their hearts were so taken up with God's that they prayed and planned and dreamed about how they could quench the need that so troubled their souls. In New Testament terms, I believe that the joy behind their sacrifice is what we refer to as grace.

Read 2 Corinthians 8:1-4. According to verse 1, what was given to the Macedonian churches and who gave it?

What were the effects of this gift?

Now read verses 8-12. According to verse 10, the Corinthians (the people Paul was writing to) were not only the first to give but the first to have the _____ to do so.

The greek word is *thelo*, and it means *to will, decide, want to; wish, desire.* Think of how different thelo is from begrudging, dreading, reluctantly offering, giving out of guilt, dutifully showing up. The difference between thelo and every other form of self-originating desire can only be the grace of God. The desire Nehemiah had in his heart to rebuild the wall in Jerusalem was initiated by God (see Neh. 2:12). When David longed to build God a dwelling place for His Name, God reshaped the vision and fulfilled the promise by His own power (see 1 Kings 8:15). And when Paul wrote to the Corinthians reminding them of the generosity of the Macedonian church, he referred to the grace of God as the catalyst behind their longing to give (see 2 Cor. 8:1).

FUN FACT: NEHEMIAH IS ONE OF THE LAST BOOKS OF THE OLD TESTAMENT, ENDING ABOUT 400 YEARS BEFORE CHRIST.

PERSONAL RESPONSE: What has God put in your heart to do? Write down passages of Scripture that come to mind, longings you have for others, people you want to reach out to.

Now that you've recorded your thoughts, consider committing to a season of prayer regarding what God is laying on your heart. If you don't sense anything at the moment, keep asking Him to show you. I cannot overstate how excited I am for you to experience the joy of tangibly sacrificing for those God has put around you or maybe even overseas. I write these words with great humility aware that my involvement with the poor, needy, sick, or uneducated has always been God's initiation and the unrivaled joy of my life. We'll come back to this Personal Response throughout our study so you can continue to develop it as God reveals His vision to you. May you one day hear the words, "You have done well to have this in your heart."

LAURI'S
BEEF ENCHILADAS

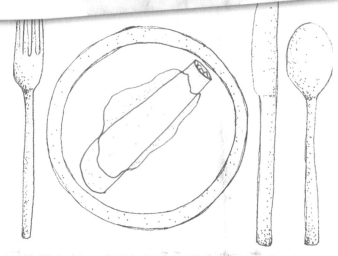

This is an all-time Lauri special. She cooked it one night for the nogs and we've never been the same.

SERVES 4

1 lb. ground beef
3 tablespoons oil, divided
1/4 cup flour
1 teaspoon tomato paste
8 oz. shredded
  cheddar cheese
1 onion
2 cloves garlic
2 tablespoons chili powder
2 dried ancho pepper
  (or other dried pepper)
14 oz. broth
  (beef or chicken)
1 cup water
12 corn tortillas (small)
8x8-inch square pan
food processor

DIRECTIONS: To make the sauce toast peppers in a pan, remove and take out seeds and stems. Rehydrate by putting in bowl and covering with water, let sit 10 minutes. Put in food processor, add water until paste forms, set aside. In pan put 2 tablespoons oil and heat. Add 1/4 cup flour and whisk. Pour in broth and water, chili powder, and paste. Salt to taste and whisk until boiling. Reduce.

Heat another pan with 1 tablespoon oil. Add chopped onion and garlic, lightly saute until onions are translucent. Add ground beef and cook until done. Add salt and pepper.

Heat oven to 350 degrees, wrap tortillas in foil and cook until pliable (about 10 minutes). Pour a little sauce in square pan. Put beef and cheese in tortilla, roll and layer. Pour sauce over each layer and whatever is left on top. Sprinkle with cheese. Turn oven up to 400 degrees and cook until cheese is melted and bubbly (about 20 minutes).

MOM'S
GINGER SNAPS

3/4 cup butter

1 cup brown sugar

1 egg

1/4 cup molasses
   (use real molasses with no extras)

2 1/4 cup flour

2 teaspoons baking soda

1 teaspoon cinnamon

1 teaspoon ginger

1/2 teaspoon cloves

1/4 teaspoon salt

sugar for rolling

I have an addiction to ginger snap cookies. There, it has been confessed. Pair these up with a cup of tea and your group will love you. Or, if you're like me and your mom makes them for you, you will love your mom even more than you already do.

DIRECTIONS: Cream butter with brown sugar until fluffy (with a hand mixer). Then beat in the egg. Add molasses. Put the next 6 dry ingredients in a separate bowl and mix well. Add to creamed mixture. Make into balls and roll them in sugar. Bake at 350 degrees for 10 minutes or until lightly browned. Don't overbake, if you want them chewy in the middle and crunchy on the outside.

The Discovery, Ray of Hope's boat in Brazil
(See Kelly's sister Katie share her Amazon experience on session 2 video.)

SESSION 2
COME TOGETHER

I DECIDED TO START CANNING TOMATOES SO I COULD READILY ACCESS THE FLAVORS OF SUMMER IN TASTELESS MONTHS LIKE FEBRUARY; AT LEAST THIS WAS WHY I INITIALLY THOUGHT I WANTED TO CAN. I KNOW YOU CAN BUY CANS OF TOMATOES AT THE GROCERY STORE YEAR-ROUND—MY FRIENDS REMIND ME OF THIS ALL THE TIME—BUT WHERE'S THE HEART AND PERSONAL RISK IN THIS?

Like cooking, canning requires a certain commitment, only the stakes are much higher when you can. If you get canning wrong you can end up with a funny little bacteria called *botulism*, meaning you could die over a plate of linguini. This terrified me, which is why I went for broke and bought a pressure canner—a large aluminum pot that can reach superheated temperatures and quite possibly build up enough steam to launch a rocket to Uruguay. Ironically this life-threatening pot is a weapon with which you can waltz right out of the cookware aisle.

The first time I tried out my pressure canner I watched for steam to escape through a small vent pipe on the lid, at which point I placed a small pressure regulator on top of it. You're supposed to wait until the steam inside the canner builds up enough pressure to move the regulator back and forth, and, incidentally, this takes more time than you might think. Figuring I'd probably botched the whole procedure I decided to start over and pulled the regulator off. This was a grave error. What transcended was a release of steam that shot like a laser beam to the ceiling in a shrieking howl that threw me to the kitchen floor.

After that little number I put the weight back on and finally it started moving in—what was supposed to be—a "gentle, rocking motion," though mine was rattling like a train was about to plow through the lid. I cowered from a distance, watching the whole contraption hoot and holler on my stove top, wondering if the dangers of pressure canning had surpassed the dangers of botulism—what's a little bacteria compared to blowing myself up in my own home?

This was just the processing part. Don't get me started on the bushels of tomatoes I'd hauled in from the farmers' market—the ones I'd blanched, dipped in ice water, peeled, cored, and funneled into a jar all by myself. My friends suddenly had "other" things to do like sweep under their beds. Hundreds of tomatoes in wooden baskets overtook my dining room table and countertops, plenty for what I perceived could keep all of Italy cranking for at least a couple months. It wasn't until I checked the directions, and realized it takes about 45 pounds of tomatoes to make approximately 7 quarts of sauce, that I began to question the path my life was on.

It was then that I roughly priced out my hard and soft costs: pressure canner, canning supplies, tomatoes, lemons for lemon juice, salt, suffering, and overall trauma. Based on rough configurations my jars of tomatoes came to about $73 a piece, if you keep health insurance out of it.

Further troubling was that I didn't process the first seven jars correctly (add additional "learning-curve expense"). The lids sealed so they were most likely "safe" to eat, but tossing them felt like prudence so I set them aside. The next day my exceedingly helpful friend April came over and, without me knowing, put away all the jars in the pantry, in other words mixing good jars with possibly tainted ones. This created a scenario called Tomato Russian Roulette—don't know if you've ever heard of it—which we played until all the tomatoes had been eaten.

Whenever I opened my pantry I happily stared at the rows of jewel-red jars, despite the underlying possibility of severe illness. Each one was like a little quart of gold to me, though more expensive than gold mind you. They made me feel settled and homey, like I lived in the old days when people used to sway on their porch swings while shucking corn and talking about how the neighbors' chickens got out of their coup. Popping open a lid was like freeing the taste of August into the dead of winter, and this lured guests into my home. It was these guests who made all my canning toils disappear into soups, sauces, and chili, especially when they would say something like, "This is the best sauce *ever!*" And I would say, "Oh, it's probably because I can my own tomatoes. It's nothing really." Then we'd sit down and eat and converse and share life together. And I would totally forget I'd almost died.

IT TOOK SOME ANALYZING TO DISCOVER, BUT THE REAL REASON I STARTED CANNING IS BECAUSE I'M DEEPLY RELATIONAL. IN THE END, CANNING WAS ABOUT DINNER AND DINNER WAS ABOUT CONVERSATION AND COMMUNITY AND TOGETHERNESS.

Which is why the week we're about to explore is one of my favorites because all types of people— young, rich, city folk, farmers, old, rulers, servants, merchants, priests, and women—will join Nehemiah in a grand endeavor they will undertake together. It will make all of Nehemiah's solitary praying, petitioning, and assessing mean so much more. Because the trip he is about to take to Jerusalem was never really about stones or gates but about the community those fortifications would protect. Be it canning tomatoes or building walls, it's all about the people.

VIDEO 2

NOTES:

_____

_____

_____

_____

_____

_____

_____

_____

_____

_____

How has today's teaching caused you to think differently about repentance? (See Neh. 1:6-7.)

In what ways does personal repentance free you from constantly focusing on the sin and shortcomings of others?

How did Katie's story impact the way you think about repentance? What impacted you the most?

Video sessions are available for download at *www.lifeway.com/women*

DAY 01

ASSESSING THE NEED

Summer nears, enticing me with visions of succulent heirloom tomatoes lining the side of my house in a valiant row of edible architecture that gets the perfect amount of sun and protective shade. I have plans for squash and zucchini, though I hear if you have even HALF a plan for squash they will proliferate and overtake your life—if there's ever a shortage of squash in the world, the end is near. I would like to pluck onions from the ground that I can use in that evening's meal or simply add to the previously harvested mound that sits in a dark cool space in my pantry. I see shoots of garlic hanging in my kitchen, their stalks wound together in culinary braids. I have dreams of raised beds made from nontreated railroad ties that are equal parts productive and aesthetic.

Of course all this is vain imagination. Right now I have nothing but a cleared backyard and a book called *The Vegetable Gardener's Bible* my friend Lisa gave me. But I'm earmarking pages and researching exciting things like compost piles. I'm watching documentaries on eating locally, and with each new slice of information I'm carried closer to my imaginary garden becoming a reality where all will be welcome to come by for squash.

Executing one's vision demands thoughtful assessment and proper planning. Though my plans for shiny eggplants don't compare with Nehemiah's zeal to rebuild the wall of Jerusalem, reach with me out of kindness. Nehemiah had a vision to rebuild the walls, but how to execute the vision required research and investigation. He needed to know what he was up against before he could unveil his plan. He had some assessments to make, which I want you to read about in Nehemiah 2:11-20.

What was Nehemiah doing in the middle of the night (see v. 13)?

A working picture of Jerusalem's walls will help us see the parts Nehemiah scouted during his first few days in Jerusalem. Though we don't know precisely where everything was located, scholars have come up with some pretty good renditions. See the map on page 44, which you will complete on day 2 this week.

Nehemiah knew that the wall had to be rebuilt, but until he assessed the damage and examined the degree of brokenness he couldn't begin to know what that job would entail. Jesus speaks to this same principle when describing the cost of being His disciple in Luke 14:28-33.

PERSONAL TAKE: Reread Nehemiah 2:16. Why do you think Nehemiah kept his mission a secret at first?

What might have happened if he'd told of his idea too early?

PERSONAL RESPONSE: Last week we ended with a prayerful time of pondering what God has put in your heart. Has He shown you additional parts of that vision? Write about them in the margin.

Nehemiah had been the wise caretaker of the plan God put in his heart. He had fostered and sculpted it during his four months of prayer and planning, he had delicately laid it before the king, and now he was ushering it into Jerusalem under the tight cover of his heart. He would keep it a secret until it became clear that the time had arrived for him to unveil his plan. As Kidner said so perfectly, "He would have lost this [initiative] if he had been exposing half-formed ideas piecemeal to every acquaintance."[1] Um, why does it sound like Kidner has met me?

I am excellent at keeping a secret someone has entrusted to me, but when God has laid something on my heart that I am excited about, I tend to wing it out there sometimes too quickly. I can be a glutton for immediate feedback and other people's reactions. Discussing things over with trustworthy people is a wonderful gift, but sometimes God drops a dream in our hearts that we must pray over and develop, that we must cultivate by His Word and direction before we share it with others. Here we get a beautiful example from Nehemiah who nurtured a seed of vision into a fully recognizable bloom, before making it known. In verses 17-18 Nehemiah revealed his plan to the people.

What compelling reason did he give at the end of verse 17 for why the wall should be rebuilt?

This is exactly what upset Nehemiah so much in 1:3. It wasn't just the suffering of the people but the disgrace of a city that, according to Psalm 48:2, was supposed to be the joy of the whole earth, the city of the Great King! Things were not the way they were supposed to be. Certainly we live in a different time, even under a different covenant. But the principles carry beyond Nehemiah's day. Disgraces, tragedies, and abuses take place all around us—things that should not be. God's church is to work at setting things right as we seek His kingdom here on earth.

As Nehemiah's heart broke over Jerusalem's disgrace, ours should break for the disgrace of the poor, abused, abandoned, and lost. Especially for those who may not appear disgraced in their put-together outfits and sewn-up facades but who are tormented with shame on the inside. As New Testament believers we recognize that our task is not to rebuild the physical city of God's dwelling place but to bring restoration to people's hearts through Jesus Christ who takes away our sin and shame.

///

GROUP DISCUSSION:
Have you ever forced a plan or a dream that, in retrospect, you realized God's hand wasn't on? If so, what did you learn from this experience?

God no longer dwells in a physical temple but where? (See 1 Cor. 3:16-17; Col 1:27.) Respond in the margin.

Nehemiah had to convince the people that rebuilding the wall was a worthy cause, and he didn't do this from a distance. In 2:17: *"You* see the trouble *we* are in. … Come, let *us* rebuild." Nehemiah didn't merely send help from Persia, but he chose to share in their suffering and recovery process. We can't miss this extreme display of sacrifice as we consider how we are identifying with the poor and suffering in our own lives.

For such a massive undertaking, Nehemiah had to make the case that Yahweh was unmistakably involved. How did he do this in verse 18?

How had God already demonstrated His involvement (see v. 8)?

Nehemiah knew without a doubt that God had given him the vision to rebuild and His gracious hand was upon him with every step. This makes all the difference when tackling something that's beyond our natural strength because if we're not assured of God's presence we will find a thousand reasonable opportunities to turn back.

How did the people respond to Nehemiah's plan in verse 18?

○ reluctantly   ○ favorably

○ with skepticism   ○ with indifference

Reread verses 19-20 and fill in the missing information about Nehemiah's prominent enemies.

_____, the Arab; Tobiah, the _____; and _____, the Horonite

We'll learn more about these characters in the days to come, but that opposition would follow the Jews' decision to rebuild the walls of the city, where God's Name dwelt, is no surprise. For now, let's look at Nehemiah's response to them.

What did Nehemiah say God would do?

What did he say he and the Jews would do?

True / False: Nehemiah encouraged the opposition to take part in rebuilding if only they stopped their attacks.

I love Nehemiah's response as much for what he didn't say as for what he did. I can't believe he didn't whip out his building permit from King Artaxerxes like an FBI agent flashes his badge. But when Nehemiah spoke, he only credited the God of heaven for his future success (see 1:5). He saw God's hand as far superior in moving Jerusalem forward and in dealing with Sanballat, Tobiah, and Geshem. Nehemiah didn't mention his military escort or the backing he'd received from Persia; only God's favor, God's people, and the distinction of Jerusalem. Brilliant.

PERSONAL RESPONSE: In what situation do you desperately need God's hand? Where are you leaning on your own resources?

As I think about Nehemiah's response to opposition, I think of my desperate need for God in all areas of my life. I don't write a lot about my singleness, at least not in the sense of it being an incomplete stage of life, or worse yet, a nonmedical disease. (Plus, it tends to set off a frantic alarm in women who suddenly have an unruly urge to set me up with their son, cousin, or uncle they haven't seen in 15 years, *but who really loves the Lord*. I write in love.) But in the last few months I have become very aware of how much I take care of myself.

My dream was never to do life without someone committed to walking alongside me until death do us part. I have friends who are as tight as family. My life is filled to the brim with joy and adventure, but only a man can fill the roll of a man in my life. Some days I wake up and say, "Lord, be my husband, my father, my brother," even though I have the best father and brother ever, they just don't live close enough to mow my lawn. I long for the faith of Nehemiah who looked the opposition dead in the eye and said, "I've got God." And, by the way, He trumps everything.

DAY 02

CITY GATES, SOUL GATES

When projects turn overwhelming and the obstacles loom, camaraderie rolls the windows down and gets the breeze blowing, reminding us that everyone's in this thing together. During my winter trip to the Amazon I had the joy of working with a team and benefiting from everyone's gifts and personalities. My dad taught the jungle pastors on the veranda while my friends Warren and Mike oversaw the builders. Now, my father is a man of the Scriptures and an exquisite teacher, but please don't allow him to touch a hammer. If your toilet overflows, he will tell you to pray about it. Conversely, none of us could have preached for five hours at a time without a note, fielding questions with humble ease from phenomenal men of a different culture.

While builders built and teachers taught, my friend Jaye made home visits, sidestepping religious and cultural minefields, moving straight to the hearts of perfect strangers with a graceful authority that would astound you. Come evening, Brad, dropped his drill for a gaggle of little boys and girls who followed him around like the Pied Piper. At any moment you might have seen Juliet, my dear English friend, drawing tanned, weary hands to her chest, praying comforting prayers over women desperate for a touch from God. Occasionally I would pick up my guitar and lead deep and theologically complex songs like Father Abraham (LEFT FOOT, RIGHT FOOT, TURN AROUND ...). So few can do what I do.

In the end, we all made way for one another's gifts. Joy upon joy came from doing it together.

Today we enter a new phase in the Book of Nehemiah. One scholar commented that chapters 1–2 describe the "innovation process" while chapters 3–7:4 describe the "community development process."[2] Up until this point Nehemiah had been defining his vision and preparing for its execution, but now the time had come for the work to begin. This he could not do alone. Take time to read Nehemiah 3:1-15.

Chapter 3 mentions at least 40 sections of the wall, but today we'll primarily focus on the gates discussed in the first 15 verses. We will gather geographical information and identify a few notable people, reminding ourselves that this was a real wall built by real people.

> **Look at the map on page 44. In the blanks, fill in the name of each gate and tower according to the given reference.**
>
> **What phrase is repeatedly used to describe the repairs made to each gate? (Phrase found in vv. 3,6,13-15.)**

I didn't notice the repetition of this phrase until months into studying Nehemiah. Once recognizing it, I had to ponder its profound significance: Little is as important to a city as guarding the places where people come and go. Jerusalem's walls meant nothing without fortified gates—every door, bolt, and bar had to be scrutinized and secured. This led me to think about the "gates" in my life, what I allow to enter my seeing and hearing, even what I taste and touch. I thought about the gates mothers and fathers are in charge of overseeing for the sake of their children. The question became, "What am I allowing in and out?"

Have you ever wondered if "mindless entertainment" might actually be a wide-open gate in your life by which many hurtful and deceiving ideas are sliding straight into your thinking? What about the friendships you keep, the magazines you read, the conversations in which you choose to engage? Are your doors open to the uplifting, truth-telling, and life-giving, or to what corrodes your soul? All day long we choose what goes in and out of our hearts and minds, and if you're like me there are some doors, bars, and bolts that need tightening.

///
GROUP DISCUSSION:
Discuss your best experience working with a team. Whose skills and personality did you especially appreciate? What did everyone accomplish by working together?

nehemiah's Jerusalem

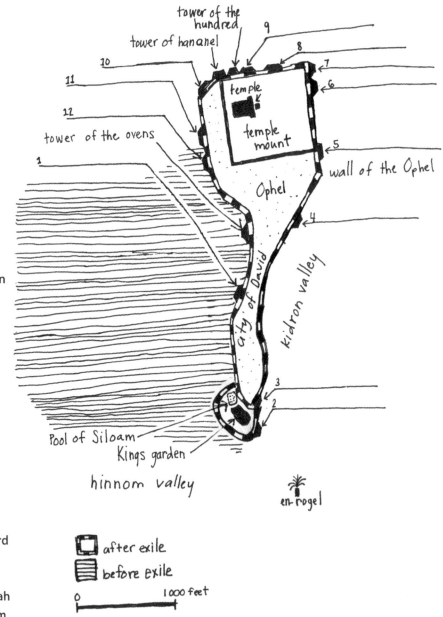

tower of the hundred

tower of hananel

tower of the ovens

temple

temple mount

Ophel

wall of the Ophel

city of David

kidron valley

Pool of Siloam

Kings garden

hinnom valley

en-rogel

after exile

before exile

0   1000 feet

ON THE MAP:
Fill in the gates
of Jerusalem as
numbered,
beginning with
those mentioned in
Nehemiah 2:13-15.
Note several
locations are
approximate or
subject to debate.

1. Valley Gate
2. Dung Gate
3. Fountain Gate
4. Water Gate
5. Horse Gate
6. Inspection Gate
7. East Gate
8. Gate of the Guard
9. Sheep Gate
10. Fish Gate
11. Gate of Jeshanah
12. Gate of Ephraim

Just as the Jews were called to guard their city, so we are called to guard our hearts. Keep considering this connection as we continue to study the rebuilding of Jerusalem's walls and gates.

Nehemiah 3:5 breaks from the consistently positive narrative of eager workers and mentions a resistant group. Who were they?

○ servants
○ nobles
○ women and children
○ foreigners

Tekoa (home of the prophet Amos) was located southeast of Bethlehem near the area controlled by Geshem. These nobles may have feared getting involved in the work based on their close proximity to enemy territory, though we can't be sure. In any case, it's discouraging to see that not everyone was onboard though a good leader understands that the work can't be stopped because a few oppose or refuse to be involved. I'm that person who doesn't like to move forward without everyone's support and approval, but this can be idealistic and maybe a tiny bit codependent. The Lord helped break me of this during a difficult situation where being obedient to Him meant walking alone. ✚

+

PERSONAL REFLECTION: What about you? Is it hard for you to move forward without everyone's support or approval? Why or Why not?

What trades are associated with the following men (v. 8)?

Uzziel: _____ Hananiah: _____

Many engaged in the work based on family or geographical ties, but some came together based on their specific trades. People who have refined their skills fascinate me because the investment of developing one is so steep; years of studying and practice go into honing a craft. You can't buy the skill of piano playing like you can buy the piano.

PERSONAL REFLECTION: If you could have any trade or skill, what would it be and why?

Though we should all be intent on using our specific gifts and trades for the service of God, sometimes we have to meet a need whether we're suited for the job or not. This was true of the goldsmith, perfumers, and merchants (mentioned later) who worked to rebuild Jerusalem, even though this type of work had little to do with their skill set. They saw a need, and they took their place on the wall.

> **Look back at verse 12. With whom did Shallum repair his section of the wall? His …**
>
> ○ servants   ○ daughters
>
> ○ sons   ○ nobles

This is a profound mention given the cultural mores of the day. According to David J.A. Clines' book on Nehemiah, "The daughters were mentioned only because Shallum had no sons. There is no reason to think they were the only women involved in the construction."[3] For further explanation, read Numbers 27:1-11.

> **According to this passage, who would inherit the name and property of a father who had no sons?**

> **According to Numbers 36:8-12, what were the daughters who received the inheritance to then do?**

This scene of Shallum and his daughters working together to rebuild the city of God needs no embellishment. It is simply beautiful.

> **PERSONAL RESPONSE: If you have children, how can you involve them in missional projects? If you don't have children, how can you involve your nieces, nephews, or the children of close friends?**

Carrie writes about how she is already involving her 4 year-old, Finley. "It is so important to me for my kids to understand God's grace and have a thankful heart. We thank God every night in our prayers for giving us a bed and a house to sleep in. We talk about how some people don't have what we have. A group of us had the chance to help our church with a program called 'Room At The Inn' which gives men a bed and a warm meal for the night. It was important for me to walk my son Fin around the room where all the cots were laid out beforehand.

We talked about how the men that would use them did not have a home right now but that God loves them just like He loves all of us. I pray that this makes a visual impact on him and how we need to appreciate the bed that we take for granted every night. We need to daily look for types of teaching opportunities for our kids (and for us)!"

PERSONAL REFLECTION: Regardless of where you are, as you end today's lesson ponder 1 Corinthians 12:1-11. What gifts has the Spirit given you?

DAY 03

SIDE BY SIDE

*Sometimes it takes a catastrophe to meet your neighbor. When Nashville was pummeled by a hundred-year flood, streams of us trickled out of our houses and onto the streets. When struck by a shared hardship, unrelated people can bond in an instant over the common goal of recovery. During the flood cleanup, while rebuilding a stranger's house, I met more people from my home church than I had in the last eight years of Sunday morning attendance. With four services and minimal time between each, you're not afforded as much time to build relationships as when you're sweeping your paintbrush steadily against the trim and the person next to you is rolling, and suddenly you discover you both love real estate. Since the flood I can walk into my church at any service and find myself waving to Scott and Donna, Mildred and Gene, Andy, Tyler, Cindy, Chris, and Kitty. The funny thing is I didn't meet any of them in the walls of church but in a stranger's house **DOING** church. Side by side.*

Pray over today's study time. Ask God to reveal Himself to you.

Today's passage moves us from the western and northern parts of the wall to the eastern side. You will notice that it reads differently from yesterday's portion of Nehemiah because the landmarks are mostly personal houses and buildings instead of gates. Read Nehemiah 3:16-32 and in the margin tally the number of times "next to him," "after him," or "beside him" are used. (Try not to miss the content for the counting.)

What strikes you most about today's reading?

> AFTER HIM BARUCH SON OF ZABBAI DILIGENTLY REPAIRED ANOTHER SECTION, FROM THE ANGLE TO THE DOOR OF THE HOUSE OF ELIASHIB THE HIGH PRIEST.
>
> NEHEMIAH 3:20

Verses 20-21 tell us that Baruch and Meremoth helped make repairs on the high priest Eliashib's house. Looking back at verse 1, where had Eliashib been working?

Eliashib's unique position as a high priest required that he focus his attention on the strategically important area of the northern wall which was close to the temple. He didn't have the luxury (or he laid down the luxury) of staying home and working on the wall across from his own house. Whereas many could do the work of repairing the wall near their homes, the dedication of towers and gates required the special office of a high priest. I really love the idea of Baruch and Meremoth repairing what is of particular interest to Eliashib while he was away offering his services to the Lord on a unique part of the wall. While Eliashib was serving God, Baruch and Meremoth were serving God by serving Eliashib.

What adjective is used to describe the work of Baruch?

This translated word appears only here in Nehemiah. It means *to burn, to be earnest.* We are all called to be compassionate, kind, and zealous for the things of God (see Col. 3:12; Rom. 12:11), but our life experiences and gifts will naturally cause us to care more deeply about some things than others.

My friend Warren, the builder I mentioned yesterday, has a grandson with special needs. Barring a miracle from the Lord, his grandchild will never sit up on his own, nor will he ever be able to feed himself. Because of this difficult experience, and because of Christ's heart in Warren, he sponsors children with special needs all over the world. Like Baruch, he literally burns with compassion for them.

My friend Angie Smith (author of *I Will Carry You*) lost her beloved daughter Audrey within a few hours of giving birth. In the wake of this devastating hardship, she writes, "Too much is happening in the world for us to sit back and ignore what we are being called to, and for me that stems from my love of children."[4] I don't know what you're zealous for, but whatever it is, work at it earnestly. Because as I now like to say, "If it's not Baruch, you might want to fix it."

PERSONAL RESPONSE: In matters relating to God's kingdom, what are you most zealous about? What makes your heart burn?

If you currently feel numb and dull and can't put your finger on anything, ask God to create in you a kingdom passion. This is His will so you can feel confident praying for it.

Earlier you kept count of the references of "next to," "after," and "beside" him. How many did you come up with?

Though the catalogue of names listed in chapter 3 may seem tedious at first, it represents an extraordinary feat of organization and accomplishment and displays a beautiful picture of God's people working together to accomplish God's purposes. They did it next to one another in a display of community that makes me freshly happy our God has not called us to serve Him alone.

PERSONAL TAKE: Here is a short list of names pulled from chapter 3. Fill in their vocations in the following chart. What inspires you the most about their diversity? Respond below the chart.

NAME	VOCATION
Eliashib (see v. 1)	High Priest
Uzziel (see v. 8)	
Hananiah (see v. 8)	Perfumer
Rephaiah (see v. 9)	
Pedaiah (see vv. 25-26)	
Shemaiah (see v. 29)	

I am amazed at the organization behind getting all of these different types of people to work together with common intention and efficiency. Though a testament to Nehemiah's leadership, we don't get a "how-to" as much as a "he-did." What we will continue to discover about Nehemiah is that he did it because the hand of his great God was upon him. One thing you may have noticed is that although Nehemiah 3 contains great diversity, culturally speaking it was homogeneous; everyone was a Jew, or a proselyte who had chosen to convert. Since the coming of Christ, this has drastically changed as the gospel has spread in extraordinary directions, reaching all manner of distinctive people.

Where did Jesus call His disciples to be witnesses (see Acts 1:8)?

Who can be in Christ according to Colossians 3:11?

Some of my richest, deepest, and most hysterically funny moments have been with people from other countries, or people who are simply different from me. These relationships do more than keep me interested and entertained, they remind me of the universality of the gospel. When we come to "the wall" alongside believers who are vastly unique, our faith is deepened. Paul speaks to this gift of fellowship in 1 Thessalonians 3:10.

> **Fill in the blanks: "Night and day we pray most earnestly that we may see you again and _____ what is _____ in your _____" (NIV).**

I love the New Living Translation, which says, "to fill the gaps in your faith," much like the people were filling in the gaps in the wall.

Who consistently supplies what is lacking in your faith? How so?

To me, one of the most freeing phrases in today's reading is "each in front of his own house" (v. 28, NIV, see also vv. 29-30). There is no question that we as the body of Christ have a responsibility to those living beyond our immediate spheres, and yet there is much work to be done right where we've been planted: in our work environments, communities, neighborhoods, schools, churches, and families. God may be calling you to serve in the places that are right in front of your own home! I love how scholar H.G.M. Williamson puts it: "It seems that Nehemiah allowed each group to be responsible, so far as possible, for the section of the wall in which *they had the greatest vested interest*—because it protected their home, place of business, or the like. … [We need not] be disquieted if we find that it *comes most easily, and with the greatest sense of motivation, to channel those gifts in areas closest to our own concerns*" (emphasis added).[5]

> **Read 1 Corinthians 12:12-27, keeping Nehemiah 3 in mind. Let Paul's words encourage you as you consider how you are investing in the body of Christ. Respond below.**

DAY 04
ENTER THE OPPOSITION

I've learned something significant about myself in the past few months: I hate confrontation more than meatloaf. It's been an unusual season of opposition that's made me long for someone to pass the reins off to, and if that person happens to be an attractive single man, well then chime the wedding bells. Until then the Lord is teaching me to trust Him as my Defender while making me tougher. Sometimes you have to draw back, keep quiet, and pray, but I'm learning that other times God asks you to get out there and stand your ground. Today and throughout the Book of Nehemiah we'll witness a biblical blend of both. Read Nehemiah 4:1-6.

What part of opposition bothers you the most? Why?

Up to now the enemies' threats have been more annoying than effective at interrupting the work. But this is the first time we're told that Sanballat had shown up in person, bringing his allies with him. When looking at our opposition it's helpful to understand the reason behind their angst.

According to verse 1, why were the Jews' enemies so upset?

Based on the multitude of enemies confronting the Jews, Jerusalem's situation brings fresh meaning to the phrase, "opposed on every side."

Sanballat was governor of Samaria which was to the north of Jerusalem. Tobiah is believed to have held a high office in the land of Ammon, which sat to the east of Jerusalem. Geshem is thought to have ruled a host of Arabian tribes which ruled over Moab, Edom, and Arabia, which were Judah's neighbors to the east and south. The Ashdodites were the Jews' western neighbor.

PERSONAL RESPONSE: Think about a time when you felt attacked from every side. What did you learn from this season, and how did it affect your relationship with God?

Don't miss how angry and incensed Sanballat had become when he found out that the wall was progressing. The literal translation is to "become hot" and "be angry," and when used together in this particular form the intent is to relay intense, raging anger.[6] Sanballat's territory was being threatened by the promise of a restored Jerusalem, and when people are threatened they tend to go straight for the throat. Out of control rage does not heed reason or common courtesy, which is why Sanballat attacked the Jews where they were most vulnerable.

+

PERSONAL REFLECTION:
Think about what half-truths leveled at you have hurt you the most. Why do you think the wounds that carry a shard of truth are the most painful?

> **Fill in Sanballat's missing word: What are those _____ Jews doing? (See Neh. 4:2.)**

These fighting words stood to puree the Jews' confidence because they held just enough truth to be devastating.

> **Look up Deuteronomy 7:1,6-8, and answer the following:**
>
> **True / False: The Israelites inherited the promised land because they were bigger and stronger than five of the seven nations they were told to drive out.**
>
> **True / False: God chose Israel as His treasured possession, even though they were the fewest of all peoples.**

In the entire Old Testament the word "pathetic" (HCSB) or "feeble" (NIV) appears only here, and Sanballat was the one to hurl it against God's people while his sidekick Tobiah tossed out jokes about a fox toppling a 9-foot thick wall. They remind me of the two old men from the Muppets who wisecracked from the safety of their theater booth, only meaner. They had yet to shoot an arrow but the dart of words had been fired, and from Nehemiah's response in verses 4-5 we see that he and the Jews took it to heart, "Listen, our God, for *we are despised*" (emphasis added). ✚

Words can be the most damaging thorns pressed into our hearts, often hurting far more than any physical blow. The Jews were well aware that they were not known for their size or strength; with opposing leaders and an army now forcefully reminding them of this, they needed to hear from God. So Nehemiah prayed.

In an escalating situation like this, prayer doesn't always feel like the fastest or most efficient solution. We're accustomed, even trained, to look to our resources first, wrack our brains, and at the very least Google our problems for some immediate answers. We want quick remedies for our quandaries and our suffering. But this is where Nehemiah provides an encouraging example. God was always His first stop; action always followed, it never led. Look at the following three couplets of obedience and action: "So I prayed. 'If it pleases the king … send me' " (2:4-5). "The God of heaven is the One who will grant us success. We, His servants, will start building" (2:20). "Listen, our God. … So we rebuilt the wall. … We prayed to our God and stationed a guard" (4:4-9). ✚

Will you commit to petitioning the Lord about this situation for at least the remainder of our study?

How did the people work according to Nehemiah 4:6?

+

PERSONAL REFLECTION: Write about something to which you've applied your resources, brain power, or finances but haven't spent sig-nificant time praying about.

The potential effectiveness of the verbal assaults stopping the work was diverted by prayer and the people's willingness to work with all their hearts. The Lord also had given them wisdom about how to proceed.

According to verse 6, how high did they build the wall, and how much of it was built to this height? Answer in the margin.

So instead of completing the sections that were easily coming along and leaving the more difficult chunks for later, they decided to get the whole wall to the halfway mark. This may have meant leaving certain portions that were well-along in order to fill the gaps that were leaving vulnerable holes. It was better for the whole wall to be shored up, even though incomplete, than to have fully built sections here and there while others lie disconnected. This feels like divine wisdom to me.

Had this wall been up to me, I would have held my megaphone shouting opposite directions like, "Let's finish up what's working and leave what's not working for later—chips and salsa at my house!" The way they chose to move forward really ministers to me right now because I am desperate for God's wisdom in some specific areas of my life. According to James 1:5, He gives it generously to those who ask.

If only this chapter ended right here with the Jews successfully rebuilding despite the intimidating insults of Sanballat, Tobiah, and the rest of them. But the story keeps going, and the enemies don't fatigue as easily as we'd hope. Continue reading verses 7-9.

After Israel's enemies saw that their verbal threats had gone unheeded, what new measures did they plot to undertake?

If damaging words cause us devastating pain, physical threats cause downright fear. If we need God's healing truth for the former, we need His physical defense for the latter. Now that Sanballat and Company had upped the ante by threatening a physical attack, suddenly the work on the wall loomed large and unlikely. But Nehemiah responded with prayer … and a plan of action, which we are finding to be his *modus operandi.*

According to verse 9, what was Nehemiah's twofold response:

When major opposition comes our way, it's essential to know we're in the right place, doing the right thing. This will give us strength in our weariness and confidence in our fear. Nehemiah's vision wasn't shaken because he was convinced of what God had put in his heart to do. He knew what the Old Testament law and the prophets had to say about the significance of Jerusalem and therefore knew that his work was founded in accordance with God's will. After all, how could it not be of God to rebuild the very city where His name and people dwelled?

There have been times in my life when I've had difficulty discerning between opposition and God's discipline. Just because we're enduring a lot of hardship and onslaughts doesn't necessarily mean we're "suffering for doing good." Sometimes we're suffering for sticking our finger in the socket. When we're disobedient, natural consequences result, along with God's loving hand of discipline. Though these consequences may feel like enemy opposition, they're not the same thing.

On the other hand, you may be dead in the center of God's will and experiencing great attack, much like the Jews who were rebuilding the wall. If so, you must renew your confidence in God, even reminding Him of His promises to you, rehearsing the threats coming against you and your work: "They have thrown insults in the face of the builders" (v. 5, NIV). Take heart that you're on exactly the right road doing exactly the right thing. ✚

> Look back at what you wrote about Nehemiah's twofold response in verse 9. What did he post day and night?

When it comes to our opposition it appears that a good defense is often as effective as a blistering offense. Being on guard can sometimes lack the excitement of blowing things up and shooting things out of cannons, it's more staid than being on offense. It's an easy concept to overlook as it tends to lack flash and commotion. No one likes to be the one to stay back. But the Bible has a lot to say about being on guard and what things warrant guarding.

> Next to each Scripture reference, briefly write what we're to guard.
>
> 1 Timothy 6:20
>
>
> Proverbs 4:23
>
>
> Proverbs 4:13
>
>
> Luke 12:1

There is a lot worth guarding in our lives, our hearts being one of the most significant. As you ponder what ways you need to shore up the protection over what God has entrusted to you, remember that He does not leave you alone. As we are guarding what He has entrusted to us, He is guarding us. "The peace of God, which surpasses every thought, will guard your hearts and minds in Christ Jesus" (Phil 4:7).

///
GROUP DISCUSSION: How has knowing you were in the will of God helped you endure difficult opposition?

➕
PERSONAL REFLECTION: If you're currently experiencing opposition, list the reasons why you still know you're on the right path. Use Scripture and confirmations the Lord has given you.

DAY 05

REMOVING THE RUBBLE

After the Nashville flood I helped rebuild three homes, and during the process I learned a worthy lesson: *The difference between building and rebuilding is rubble.* Building starts with a clean slate and means new, freshly-scented materials. Rebuilding means maneuvering through piles of brick, metal, and junk before you get to hanging the stunning chandelier you found for half-price, the one God ordained for you to own before the foundation of the world. Read Nehemiah 4:10-15.

> Fill in the following from verse 10: "The _____ of the laborer fails, since there is so much _____. We will never be able to rebuild the wall."

Rebuilding means hauling stuff away and sorting through unruly piles, salvaging the keepers from the throwaways. While looking after the rebuilding of these homes, I got excited about the new granite countertops, the fresh paint, and the pristine cabinets. If I happened to be less riveted by the moldy drywall, water-logged couches, and trips to the dumpster, well then that was my problem, because this was a *re*build not a build. Rubble bridges the great divide between the two.

Rubble threatened to stop the laborers in Jerusalem dead in their tracks. Forget Sanballat's nasty threats; forget the Ammonites who were planning to fight against them. It was that exhausting rubble that just about took them down.

> What rubble in your life is presently the most discouraging and exhausting? (For example, finances, addictions, or relationships.)

The problem with rubble is that it hangs around well after the initial destruction. Though the attack on Jerusalem's walls had long since passed, the rubble was still present. But the Jews were dealing with it, and this is the good news. Similarly, it's important for us to deal with our personal rubble or we may find ourselves still climbing over it 30 years from now. How can we properly rebuild if we never address our rubble? Getting rid of rubble requires we *do* something.

What new and harrowing threat did the enemy launch? (See v. 11.)
○ We will take them captive.
○ We will think up more jokes about their wall.
○ We will kill them.
○ All of the above.

What group of well-meaning people repeated this threat over and over to the laborers? (See v. 12.)

You may remember that King Artaxerxes had officially authorized the Jews to rebuild Jerusalem's walls, so the question naturally arises, *How can their enemies do this? This is illegal!* One thing I'm beginning to understand is that not everyone cares about what's legal or not, what's right or wrong. It's possible that Sanballat and his allies thought if they acted quickly enough there would be little the king of Persia could do. Or perhaps they were hoping the king's authorization would eventually be reversed, as had happened before.

What was ordered in Ezra 4:21-24?

Most of the Jews working on the wall in Nehemiah's day probably lived through the decree in Ezra. They had already experienced the despair of their work being stopped. When we've experienced past hardship we can easily let that precedent rule our present. We can all imagine the roads the Jews' minds may have taken them down during these trying threats. They may have viewed defeat as a foregone conclusion.

Jews from the surrounding areas turned into ancient-day re-Tweeters of Sanballat's threats (see Neh. 4:12). These concerned relatives and villagers knew that anyone who left the wall and returned to their towns would no longer be in trouble. That's why they urged the workers "time and again" to come home.[7]

You can imagine the scene: The perfume-maker's mother scurries into town and says, "Come off the wall, Son. They're going to kill you! Come back to your potentially lucrative trade; Chanel No. 5 hasn't been invented yet!" Or maybe Shallum's brother traveled in and said, "You're being reckless with my nieces! Haven't you heard the threat? Get them off the wall." Or what about the friends of the priests? "Eliashib! What use is your priesthood if you're dead?"

I believe the Jews from the surrounding areas were loving and concerned citizens, but they had lost sight of what was most important: The successful rebuild of Jerusalem. Even well-meaning people can unintentionally draw us away from God's will in our lives.

> **Nehemiah, however, had not forgotten what God had put in his heart to do. So instead of succumbing to the threats and stopping the work, what did he propose in verse 13?**

> **Write out Nehemiah's quote in verse 14.**

Nehemiah prescribed a very specific remedy for their fear: "Remember the … LORD." The laborers found themselves at the wearying halfway point that coincided with dizzying threats from their enemies that were being emphasized by their fellow townsfolk. The workers were discouraged, exhausted, and afraid.

> **PERSONAL REFLECTION: Given this information, why do you think Nehemiah's appeal to fight for their families and homes was particularly wise?**

I love that Nehemiah stationed family members together while reminding them of who it was they were fighting for in the first place. After all, this project wasn't about abstract notions or lifeless stone; this project was about people. And to each mother, father, or child, it was about *his* or *her* people.

Who are *your people* who God has asked you to fight for? List their names in the margin and pray over each one.

PERSONAL TAKE: What does verse 15 say God did to Sanballat and Company's plot? What do you think this means, since we don't have a direct reference to God's intervening?

Read Nehemiah 4:16-23.
Fill in the blanks from verse 16: "_____ _____ _____ _____, half of my men did the work while the other half held spears, shields, bows, and armor."

The Jews went back to business, but they never went back to business as usual. Because of the increasing threats of their enemies, they couldn't return to work the same way as before. Only half could do the work of building, while half now did the work of providing protection. If your job was to carry materials, you could no longer use both hands because one of them needed to have a weapon in it. If you were a builder, you had the extra weight of a sword strapped to your side. And you could no longer just be a workman by day, you had to also be a guard by night. This'll knock the whistle-while-you-work right out of a person.

I wonder if you've had a "From this day on …" experience and how it has changed your life. Perhaps life hasn't resumed to the place you had hoped it would, and maybe you've had to resolve to doing some things differently. But despite what you've had to change, one thing will always remain constant: "Our God will fight for us!" (v. 20).

PERSONAL REFLECTION: What does this promise, given throughout the Bible, mean to you personally?

This has been a really interesting week of study for me, and I hope it's been as thought-provoking for you. I have a better grasp on the importance of teamwork and what it means for us as New Testament believers. I can more readily see how the excitement over a thrilling, even God-ordained, project can wane after verbal assaults and physical threats. How the rubble can get flat overwhelming, because let's face it, most of us are doing more rebuilding than building in life. How fear can pluck from the roots up the stuff God's put in your heart to do. And how even well-meaning loved ones can rehearse the reasons as to why what you're doing is not a good idea anymore.

I'm inspired by Nehemiah's unrelenting belief and trust in God, knowing that He would fulfill the vision He had given him. Without this kind of authoritative resolve, whoever would have followed him? As the apostle Paul said, "He who calls you is faithful, who also will do it" (1 Thess. 5:24).

SOUTHWEST
CHICKEN SOUP

SERVES 4 (EASILY DOUBLES)

1 (12 oz.) can salsa verde
  (You can get in it the grocery store
  or from a Mexican restaurant.)
3 cups cooked chicken
1 (15 oz.) can cannelloni beans, drained
3 cups chicken broth
2 green onions chopped
1/2 package frozen corn
1 teaspoon ground cumin (more or less to taste)
1 teaspoon chili powder (more or less to taste)
sour cream
tortilla chips

This has become a standby for me. You will love this! (Note the exclamation point at the end of that sentence.)

DIRECTIONS: Empty salsa verde into large saucepan. Cook 2 minutes over medium-high heat. Then add chicken, beans, broth, cumin, corn, and chili powder. Bring to a boil, lower heat to simmer, and cook 10 minutes, stirring occasionally. Top each bowl with onions, sour cream, and chips. Use more broth for soupier mixture.

I like to buy a whole chicken from the farmers' market, boil it, and make my own chicken broth for this soup. If you don't have that much time, buying a rotisserie chicken works well for the 3 cups of cooked chicken needed.

Kelly and her family minister together in Brazil
(See their experience on session 3 video.)

SESSION 3
A CITY NEEDS PEOPLE

"DO YOU KNOW THE NAME OF A POOR PERSON?" A YOUNG MAN IN HIS TWENTIES WHO WAS SHARING ABOUT HIS EXPERIENCES AS A MISSIONARY IN MOLDOVA POSED THE QUESTION TO ME IN CHURCH. HIS PHRASE WAS TRICKY BECAUSE IF HE'D SAID, "DO YOU CARE ABOUT THE POOR?" I MIGHT HAVE TOSSED IT IN THAT DRAWER WHERE YOU KEEP ALL THE STUFF YOU'VE HEARD A MILLION TIMES AND ARE SUPPOSED TO PONDER BUT PROBABLY WON'T DO MUCH WITH.

When he asked if I knew the *name* of a poor person he exposed a glaring gap in my Christianity: Whose name did I know? Not whose face had I passed on 21st Street on my way to grab coffee; not what homeless man had I handed a dollar for the paper he peddles at the stoplight; not what anonymous tsunami victim had received an online donation I'd made. Whose name did I know?

I was left to consider this very important question because if I didn't know the name of a poor person, I didn't really know a poor person. (This is one of the biggest problems with going to church—the possibility of getting all convicted and stuff.) I always knew that if God's heart was for anything it was for the least of these: the suffering, sick, needy, uneducated, foreigner, lost, lonely—this much was clear. And it's true that these were people I cared about, prayed for, and on whose behalf I tithed, but how many of them called me *friend?* Who had my phone number, been to dinner at my house, or sat beside me at church? Without condemnation, I had to recognize that I was someone who cared for the poor mostly from a distance but who had yet to intimately involve herself. My first step: Learn a name.

In the Law of Moses God commanded the Israelites to leave their extra sheaves, olives, and grapes for the alien, fatherless, and widow—for all the people who didn't have what the Israelites had and who didn't have the means to get what they had. At the end of this recurring command the Lord gave His people an intriguing reason for why He required this, "Remember that you were slaves in Egypt. *That is why* I command you to do this" (Deut. 24:22, NIV, emphasis added).

Didn't God want them to leave their excess food for the poor and outsider because these people were hungry, because they needed community, because they couldn't provide for themselves, because He loved them? Wasn't that why? Oh I'm sure those were all reasons, but I believe God first had to deal with that sneaky mind-set, the one that tries to trick us into thinking that when we step over a stalk of wheat to leave it for the poor we're doing something really noble, plain over-the-top gracious. That we're going above and beyond by giving away what is rightfully "ours."

The Lord was staving off this kind of thinking by saying, "Hold your fancy horses. Remember you used to be slaves too! Don't forget to tap into what that felt like." The Israelites were no strangers to poverty, oppression, or powerlessness as ones who had once been enslaved in Egypt. It was only because of God's deliverance they were now free, only because of His goodness they were blessed with flourishing fields and bursting branches. By remembering their once low estate, they were poised to welcome the foreigner, fatherless, and widow, not out of self-righteousness, guilt, or duty, but out of the love God had shown them.

Last night I served dinner to an Iraqi couple and their 2-year-old daughter, a family some of my friends and I have gotten to know. I'd hoped that chicken, broccoli, and couscous were safe selections to serve these well-dressed Middle Easterners, though I sensed I may have been pushing it with the hot apple cider—I was going for the American autumn experience, and judging by their first and only sip, this went over moderately.

As we settled around the table I asked them why they'd left Baghdad to come to America. The husband replied, "Because there are less car bombings here," and then he broke out into hysterical laughter. (Safwat's a sanguine.) His wife was less buoyant, confiding that the war had been devastating and that they'd fled here as refugees hoping to find jobs but so far without any success. My eyes welled up as she spoke because her suffering was not that of a nameless Iraqi, but it belonged to her, a real-life woman with a name, *Rida*. As the adults carried on, Rubaa fingered the icing on her cupcake and tapped her shoes on the hardwood floors, just like any other baby girl in a bright red dress who wanted the room to be enchanted with her—some things are the same everywhere.

When it was time for them to leave, Safwat shook my hand, Rubaa blew me a kiss at her mother's urging, and Rida kissed my right cheek, left cheek, and then back to my right cheek again (it's that third one I always forget). As we said our good-byes I realized what a privilege it was to know their names, because knowing their names meant I was getting to know their stories. And knowing their stories reminded me in deeply spiritual and emotional places that I, too, was once a foreigner outside of God's kingdom, but because of Christ, I am now a daughter.

AS WE SPECIFICALLY LOOK AT THE POWERLESS, OPPRESSED, AND POOR THIS WEEK, MAY WE REVEL IN GOD'S REDEMPTION OF US, AND THEN GO LEARN A NAME BECAUSE OF IT.

VIDEO 3

NOTES:

_____

_____

_____

_____

_____

_____

_____

_____

_____

Nehemiah 1:3 tells us that Jerusalem lay in disgrace. Nehemiah 2:18 explains Nehemiah planned to remove the disgrace with God's help. Discuss the ways Nehemiah's plan to deal with the disgrace encourages you to practically be a minister of reconciliation? (See 2 Cor. 5:17-21.)

Where has God removed your own disgrace? (Don't feel pressure to share beyond your comfort level.)

What spoke to you the most in the Minter family interview?

Video sessions are available for download at *www.lifeway.com/women*

DAY 01

THE POOR, GOD'S TREASURE

Today we're going to read about Jerusalem's internal struggles as our view turns from the relentless outside oppression to some surprising turmoil within. I appreciate this window into Jerusalem's struggles because so many of our personal conflicts are kindled inside our marriages, churches, family businesses, and friendships. We know too well that clashes aren't only reserved for the good guys versus the bad guys; sometimes the most difficult trials we face are within our own walls.

> Read Nehemiah 5:1-5. Verses 2, 3, and 4 each open with a group of people in need. Describe the complaints of each group:

Group 1:

Group 2:

Group 3:

Anytime a nation turns its attention toward a massive undertaking like a war or building project, other areas tend to suffer. In Israel's case, much of the focus had turned to rebuilding the wall, as well as defending that work, so it's not surprising that an issue like caring for the poor was being neglected. Add to this a famine, and Nehemiah suddenly had a serious issue to deal with, this time coming from the inside. With a trowel for the wall in one hand and a sword in the other for the enemy, Nehemiah now had to don his mediator hat to deal with his own people.

> According to verse 1, who were the suffering crying out against?

> PERSONAL TAKE: How do you think the effects of being oppressed by this group of people were distinctly different than the oppression of Sanballat and his cohorts?

Being oppressed or attacked by a brother or sister is uniquely painful. We expect enemies to wound us, but wounds from a relative or loved one inflict hurt inside the private property lines of our souls. Those closest to us have intimate access, making their wounds the most penetrating.

Imagine how excruciating it was for the oppressed Jews to be forced to sell their children into slavery to their own countrymen. Most heart-wrenching is the mention of daughters being enslaved. These daughters were being used to "pay" the creditors for what their debtors couldn't pay monetarily. What could be more deplorable than this evil coming not from Israel's expected enemies but from their Jewish brothers?

> **PERSONAL REFLECTION: Without naming names, how has the wound from a loved one or trusted friend uniquely hurt you?**

> Fill in Nehemiah 5:5: **"Some of our daughters are already enslaved, but we are _____ because our fields and vineyards belong to others."**

One of the most insidious characteristics of oppression and abuse is that it's always inflicted upon the powerless. Consider a woman who is raped, a child who is sexually abused, or a poor person who is in bondage to slavery: All have powerlessness in common. I want you to briefly see God's relationship to the powerless in both the Old and New Testaments.

In the Old Testament, King Asa declared Israel's dependence on God in a time of physical powerlessness (see margin). A friend of mine just found out that her husband has been having an affair. One tug on the thread of adultery and a 20-year marriage has unraveled like a ball of yarn. With her moderate salary and three children all staring into an uncertain future, if she feels anything at all, powerless is it. Amidst the unruly torrents of betrayal, anger, forgiveness, and overwhelming fear, she is entrusting herself to the powerful arm of God. He is truly her only hope.

> ASA CALLED TO THE LORD HIS GOD AND SAID, "LORD, THERE IS NO ONE LIKE YOU TO HELP THE POWERLESS AGAINST THE MIGHTY. HELP US, O LORD OUR GOD."
> 2 CHRONICLES 14:11

What did Jesus do for the *spiritually* powerless in Romans 5:6-8?

The Greek word for "helpless" ("powerless" in NIV) in Romans 5:6 is *astheneo.* This word caught my attention because the first half of the word looks like our English word, asthma. It means "to be weak, ill … sick, … disabled."[1] While we were powerless to get air into our spiritual lungs, Christ died for us.

PERSONAL RESPONSE: As you consider your own frailty, spend a few minutes writing in the margin the ways God has shown His power in a time of your powerlessness. Treat this like a journal entry.

Continue reading Nehemiah 5:6-11. What was Nehemiah's strong emotional response to the Jewish oppressors who were capitalizing on the desperate situation of their countrymen (verse 6)?

The Hebrew word for anger here is *hara*. It means "to burn with anger; … to rage; … contend with."[2] If you have suffered abuse, take heart in Nehemiah's intense response to such injustice. Though I'm sure the following is a breach of English and Hebrew grammar, note that Nehemiah was *very* hara.

According to verses 9-11, what did Nehemiah demand that the guilty do and stop doing?

Nehemiah refused to merely accept words of apology but required things be made right; justice had to be served. He addressed the guilty before an assembly, which was a serious action ensuring the oppressors would be held to their promises. He even made them upgrade their promises to an oath. Continue reading verses 12-13.

Who did Nehemiah summon as witnesses in verse 12?

What symbolic act did Nehemiah perform?

In my twenties I took a trip to Africa with World Vision® where I personally witnessed outlandish suffering, more than what my tidy theology knew how to handle. After tossing around a shredded tennis

ball with some impoverished children from a school World Vision supported, I found a quiet place that overlooked the Lesotho horizon. I sat there nearly tormented by whether or not God truly cared about powerlessness and injustice. And if He cared, what was He doing about it?

Nehemiah's unique demonstration, though culturally unfamiliar to us, sheds some light on the answers to these questions. See what scholar H.G.M. Williamson has to say about this:

> **With a gesture reminiscent of the prophets' "symbolic acts,"** *Nehemiah enacted a curse against any who would violate the oath just taken.* **Small personal items were carried in a fold of the long, flowing garments, and kept secure by a belt or girdle. This Nehemiah emptied out and simultaneously pronounced his threat (emphasis added).**[3]

Nehemiah visibly demonstrated what would happen to the Jewish offenders if they broke the oath to make things right with their brothers and sisters. He invoked God to literally empty them out of His house if they violated their promise. So to answer my own question, based on these verses and hundreds of others—yes, God cares deeply about injustice. In today's reading I want you to recognize *so did Nehemiah.*

Overlooking Lesotho's horizon perhaps I asked only half the right question. I should have asked myself if I cared about injustice, and if so, what was I doing about it. Isaiah 1:16-17 reads, "Stop doing evil. Learn to do what is good. Seek justice. Correct the oppressor. Defend the rights of the fatherless. Plead the widow's cause."

PERSONAL REFLECTION: Tangibly involving ourselves for the sake of justice is a biblical command. What part is God asking you to play?

That afternoon in Africa I asked the Lord, "Why not me? Why wasn't I born in the middle of this horrendous oppression and suffering?" As I sat with my knees drawn to my chest, the Lord did not give me an answer that day, but He did respond. I scribbled down what I sensed into my journal, His words too important to be erased by the passing of time. "It is not for you to know why, but because you weren't, over your whole life you have a responsibility to care for the poor."

PERSONAL RESPONSE: Revisit the Personal Response from week 1, day 5 on page 31. How is God refining and adding to what He has put in your heart to do?

DAY 02

LAYING DOWN OUR RIGHTS

In 1964, my grandfather became the 43rd superintendent of the United States Naval Academy. This meant, among other things, that my dad and his siblings had the rare privilege of living in the superintendent's mansion, a prestigious home that had its own beauty salon, staffed kitchen, and movie theater. My dad's made-to-order breakfasts were delivered to his room via pulley system. (I tried to work something out like this with my mom, but she was surprisingly disinterested.)

The family was also given an official car and driver, but to his children's dismay my grandpa rarely used it. He didn't want anyone to think he was spending the Academy's money frivolously or give the impression he was superior to anyone else. He held the Navy in such high esteem that it was literally his joy to forgo the car and driver for the deeper satisfaction of serving the Navy with integrity. The Navy's reputation meant more to him than any luxury or privilege, though he had every right to them.

Today we'll read about some privileges Nehemiah forewent for the love of the Jewish people and ultimately for the love of God. Things could get a little uncomfortable for us today, but the freedom and blessing that accompanies laying down our rights will far make up for any uneasy feelings of conviction. Read Nehemiah 5:14-19.

What new title do we read Nehemiah held in verse 14?
○ king   ○ prince   ○ governor   ○ general contractor

What privilege did Nehemiah and his men relinquish during his 12 years in charge?

As far as I can see, there were two reasons why Nehemiah waived his governor's salary along with the allotment of choice food, fine wine, and overall dignity of privilege. Write down each reason below:

Reason #1: (See end of v. 15.)

Reason #2: (See v. 18.)

Everyone expected Nehemiah to receive his salary and necessary entertainment budget from taxing the people. Since his job entailed hosting Jewish leaders, Persian officials, and foreign dignitaries, Nehemiah had the right to tax the people for these expenses. But he understood something that was pure revelation for the day in which he lived: He would honor God more by putting the welfare of the people ahead of his own gains, even if he could legally justify these privileges. Waiving his salary and never charging for entertaining 150 Jewish officials speaks to two things. First, Nehemiah had substantial personal wealth to cover these costs. Second, he had astounding integrity to look at his salary and essentially say, "If it will help my people, I don't need any more than what I already have."

This passage reminds us we were never meant to live merely by rules but by a living Spirit. Our rights don't get to be god, our privileges are never the final word. Even if we deserve what's coming to us, if the end result is not the love of God and the love of others, what lies inside the lines of permissible is no longer beneficial. This is gospel living, as opposed to a life driven by getting whatever is rightfully ours. For a New Testament perspective on this, see 1 Corinthians 9:7,10-19.

What did Paul say he had a right to reap in exchange for sowing a spiritual seed (see v. 11)?

Why did Paul give up his right to be paid (see v. 19)?

We must be careful here because neither Paul nor Nehemiah's example is meant to imply a worker should not be paid for his or her work. Paul explicitly said that those who plow should share in the harvest. Though we have every right to receive the material rewards of hard-earned work, occasionally a higher goal is worth setting those material rewards aside. In Nehemiah's case, he had every right to draw from the people's wages for his salary and entertainment allotment—the Old Testament Law was on his side. But Nehemiah knew that if he further taxed the people for his rightful allotment, they would suffer greatly. In essence, he loved the people far more than the money they could provide him.

> **PERSONAL RESPONSE: Is God asking you to lay down an entitlement in a situation where you are justified to hold onto it? If so, what do you see as the greater purpose of relinquishing this right?**

God can reward us in far greater measure than our privileges ever will. The Lord tangibly showed me this a few months ago when I was asked to return a portion of money I had rightfully earned. I went back and forth until I realized that ultimately I wanted to respond to this extraordinarily difficult person in the way that Jesus would. I do not believe being a follower of Christ means being a doormat. Such false thinking can lead us into a great deal of trouble God never intended. But in this situation the Lord was clear with me: send the money back gracefully. I was happy to hear from the Lord on this, but after the way this person had treated me this pounded my pride like a chicken breast being beat with a mallet.

Now I almost hesitate to write this next part because I never want to give the impression that God always rewards us in the same currency of what we lay down—we're not talking karma here. Sometimes our reward won't be realized in this lifetime but in heaven. Those two things said, the day I sent the check back I received an unexpected gift worth 12 times what I had returned. It was a really tender moment for me that wasn't so much about the money but about God putting His *arm around me and saying, "I've got you." If God is asking you to lay something down for the greater good, He is able to repay you lavishly. Your rights will never outrun His blessings, even if those blessings aren't revealed until heaven.*

Nehemiah relinquished much to accomplish what ultimate task in 5:16? "Instead, I devoted myself to the construction of …

If you remember from week 1 day 5, we spent an entire lesson on what God had put in Nehemiah's heart to do for Jerusalem. After verbal assaults, physical threats, discouraged laborers, abuses of power, and economic distress, Nehemiah never diverted his focus from the wall. The process may have been slowed and altered as a result of enemies and wayward citizens, but the goal never changed. This single focus of Nehemiah simultaneously convicts and inspires me as I consider the ways I am so easily drawn away from what God has put in my heart to do.

PART 1. In the margin, list the top three things that most distract you from the things God has put in your heart.

1.

I want to include Anadara's list, as I think she speaks for all of us. "I think fear, insecurity, and doubt keep me from continuing to build my 'wall' and cause me to let down my guard and give into the Enemy. The visual of *continuing to build in the face of 'x'* is really helpful to me."

2.

3.

PART 2. In the margin, list every reason you can think of why Nehemiah's completion of the wall was more important to him than securing a huge salary along with a wine and food allotment. Skim the first five chapters of Nehemiah for your answer.

I don't want us to miss the difference between Nehemiah's gentle leadership and the oppression of the previous governors and assistants who excessively taxed the people, lording their power over the Jews. When I first read the word "lorded" (NIV) in verse 15 it reminded me of Peter's instruction to spiritual leaders in 1 Peter 5:2-3, "Be shepherds of God's flock that is under your care, serving as overseers … not greedy for money, but eager to serve; *not lording* it over those entrusted to you, but being examples to the flock" (NIV, emphasis added).

I'm saddened when I hear of church leaders who are proud or arrogant, because such behavior is totally contrary to God's heart. Attitudes like this also run God-seekers out of a church building faster than a fire alarm. On the other hand, few things are as refreshing as being led by a strong yet gentle and humble leader. At two different seasons of my life I've had the great privilege of being the worship leader under two such pastors. Both David Hughes and Jeff Simmons led with a humility and eagerness to serve that did nothing but make me want to do all that they asked of me and beyond. They each respected and supported me, and I will always say it was my joy to be led by both of them.

> **PERSONAL RESPONSE: As a leader, where can you improve based on what we've read today? Remember, we're all leaders in some way. If you're a mom, you're a leader of your children. If you have anyone under you at your job, if you teach a class, if you're on a stage, if you oversee a ministry … you're a leader. Respond in margin.**

In light of today's study, I'll leave you with Matthew 22:37-40, "'Love the Lord your God with all your heart, with all your soul, and with all your mind. … Love your neighbor as yourself." It's a challenge and inspiration to recognize that "In his own brusque style, [Nehemiah] exemplified [these] two great commandments."[4]

DAY 03

FEAR AND LIES

When I wrote my last Bible study on the Book of Ruth I got to dip my brush in the watercolor of femininity and romance, using a palette of mostly pinks and linens. For the most part, Nehemiah requires a different palette. His colors remind us of armies, swords, threats, and tough leadership. This may be a color scheme we're not as used to working in, but the themes and applications of today's reading should fit soundly into even the most feminine of souls. Men and women alike know what it's like to face discouragements and setbacks, even intimidating enemies who never cease to amaze us with their varying bullets of fear and lies. The trick is to learn how to deal with condemning voices and distractions while not forsaking the work God has called us to. You can do this in high heels. Read Nehemiah 6:1-4.

What did Sanballat and Geshem want Nehemiah to do?

What reasons did Nehemiah give for why he was not willing to accommodate their request? Respond in the margin.

Determining what we should say yes to and what we need to say no to is often one of the hardest things to discern, especially since inexhaustible needs and opportunities surround us—needs that frequently fall into noble and worthwhile categories. This is why Alli's husband, Kirk, recently encouraged me to draw up a vision statement for my personal life and ministry. He explained that when you clarify who God created you to be and what He wants you to do, you can more easily determine what opportunities fit into that vision and which ones don't.

PERSONAL RESPONSE: Is the Lord asking you to say no to something so you can focus on what He's asked you to say yes to? If so, what?

The request for a meeting is a much more civil and diplomatic approach than what Nehemiah had previously encountered from Sanballat and Company. If you're anything like the people-pleaser in me you may have viewed this invitation as an olive branch, a chance to reconcile and hug. But Nehemiah astutely saw it as a distraction. God had put a task in his heart, and nothing was going to deter him from it, especially not a meeting. A dinner party maybe … but a *meeting?*

How does Nehemiah's refusal to meet with Sanballat and his company encourage you to set godly boundaries? (See vv. 3-4.)

I'm not a huge fan of the term *boundaries* because I think we have a tendency to use them to escape the ministry God has called us to. That said, sometimes we need to draw firm lines, and Nehemiah demonstrated a really solid example of this. Read Nehemiah 6:5-9.

Check every lie the unsealed letter included about Nehemiah.
○ Nehemiah and the Jews plan to set Samaria on fire.
○ They are building the wall to stage a revolt.
○ Nehemiah is planning to become king.
○ Nehemiah is losing his hair.

Nehemiah's enemies came at him from every angle: intimidation, threats of war, an invitation to a seemingly civil meeting, and now a letter full of lies. I will give them a gold star for persistence but not a thing for creativity—this is the oldest trick *ever*. So old that it was the tactic the serpent brought against Eve in the garden of Eden. Since the lies of the Enemy are some of our greatest foes, I can't help but visit Genesis 3:1-7 for just a moment. Briefly read these verses while keeping a placeholder in Nehemiah. Then compare and contrast the following.

> **What did Sanballat and the serpent try to accomplish by lying?**
>
> **Sanballat:**
>
> **Serpent:**
>
> **How did Nehemiah and Eve each respond to the lies?**
>
> **Nehemiah:**
>
> **Eve:**

I've been pondering the role of lies in my life recently, as light-hearted as this sounds. I've been thinking primarily in two categories about this: What I believe about God that's not true, and what I believe about myself that's not true. The results have been surprising, ranging from God is not helping me, to He doesn't care about my tangible needs, to something is inherently wrong with me (besides original sin), to God doesn't love me as much as He loves that really sold-out Christian in Mongolia.

One biblical approach that has been helping me is the simple act of confession, which we'll study more closely in week 5. When I realize I am believing a lie about myself or about God, I stop and pray something like, "Lord, what I believe about You (or myself) right now is not true." When

I do this, I'm simply agreeing with God about a matter. This puts me in a position to hear from Him and align myself with what is true. Of course Scripture enlightened by the Holy Spirit is our plumb line of truth here.

PERSONAL REFLECTION: What lies can you identify that you currently believe about yourself or about God? List them in the margin and confess them.

One of the greatest tactics of Satan is that he will lie to us and then try to attach us to that lie with a cord of fear—they're codependent little things those two. Perhaps this is why I am so inspired by the clarity in which Nehemiah handled himself against Sanballat's lies and how calmly we see him respond in the face of fear. Read Nehemiah 6:10-14.

Why did Shemaiah say he was encouraging Nehemiah to take refuge in the temple?

What reason did Nehemiah give for why Shemaiah encouraged him to do this? (See v. 13.)

We don't have much insight into why Nehemiah agreed to meet with Shemaiah in the first place. Possibly, as part of feigning to be a prophet, he had told Nehemiah he'd received a word from the Lord for him. We don't know for sure. What we do know is that when Nehemiah met him he quickly realized he was an impostor. Something clearly tipped Nehemiah off.

In verse 13, if Nehemiah took refuge in the temple, he would be:
○ sacrificing   ○ worshiping
○ sinning   ○ serving

Nehemiah knew Shemaiah wasn't a true prophet because hiding in the temple was a sin. Inside the temple was reserved for priests (see Num. 18:7). One could even die if he came unprepared to the holy of holies. I realize this may come across as obvious, but anytime someone encourages us to do something contrary to God's Word, we can know for certain this advice is not from God. I spell this out not only for myself but also because I just received an e-mail from a woman dating a man who's married. He's convinced her that since they both love God and since things are "over" with his wife, their relationship is perfectly sanctioned. We can allow others to talk us into almost anything when lies and fear dictate our actions. See the pattern in the following diagram.

What I believe about God is false (He's holding out on me)

Because I believe something false about God I am afraid (I'll always be alone, no one else will ever love me)

Because I am afraid I wrongly take what I need (Affair)

It's up to me to make life work (Defeat)

In Nehemiah's case, he chose obedience over fear, even though he mentions four times in chapter 6 that his enemies were trying to frighten him. The question I want us to ponder is, what were Nehemiah's enemies, including the mysterious prophetess Noadiah, trying to accomplish by inflicting fear? Today's reading reveals two reasons.

> **Complete the two objectives of Nehemiah's enemies.**
> 1. **Discourage the people in their work, so the wall would not be** _____ **(see v. 9).**
> 2. **Intimidate him, lure him to sin, and ruin his reputation so he would be** _____ **(see v. 13).**

Fear and lies originate from the Enemy, are never from God, and always have a negative goal. They attempt to destroy the person and thus the project the person is behind. In Nehemiah's case, being deceived by the enemies' lies and falling prey to overwhelming fear would have led him into sin, which would have potentially cost him his life, not to mention the prosperity of the Jews and the completion of the wall. So much was at stake, which is why Sanballat and friends pulled out their two biggest tactics: "We'll lie to him, and we'll make him afraid."

Here Nehemiah again reveals his most dramatic weapon: "But I prayed …" (v. 9, NIV). In verse 9, Nehemiah asks God to strengthen his hands. In verse 14, he asks God to "remember" (deal with) his enemies. We have access to this very same God, even able to approach Him more boldly because of Jesus (see Heb. 4:14-16).

PERSONAL RESPONSE: Take the last few minutes of today's study to put your fears before God. It may be as simple as saying, "Lord, strengthen my hands."

DAY 04

COMPLETION, JUST THE BEGINNING

Yesterday we looked at how hard Nehemiah's enemies tried to lure him into throwing everything away. Had he allowed Shemaiah's lies to overtake him with fear he might have sought a solution that would have cost him his life and destroyed the entire undertaking of rebuilding the wall. I don't think it's a coincidence that Nehemiah's enemies unleashed threats, lies, and an onslaught of intimidation when he and his people were just inches from the finish line.

> Before starting today's reading, turn back to Nehemiah 6:1 and
> jot in margin the one last thing that remained to be done.

We can't miss the significance of the timing of Tobiah and Sanballat's last-ditch effort of hiring Shemaiah to derail Nehemiah, because it happened right before the most important event to date. I want you to read about it for yourself. Read Nehemiah 6:15-16.

The idea of the enemy ratcheting up the heat against Nehemiah just days before the completion of the wall is a pattern I've seen in my own life and in the lives of others. I've known people who have made astounding progress in areas of addiction, weight loss, sexual wholeness, or fighting through a hard marriage; and right about the moment when their lives were about to bust open like an April tulip, they stopped believing God and sought a sanctuary in their past habits and old relationships. With great sadness all you can think is … *they were so close!*

This makes me wonder in what areas am I so close? It makes me want to ask God for faith not to give up and to take hold of one of the apostle Paul's goals: finishing well (see Acts 20:24; 2 Tim. 4:7). Of course, where I've fallen short, I ask the Lord to forgive me and put me back on the path, even restoring the years the locusts may have eaten (see Joel 2:25).

> **Turning our attention back to Jerusalem's wall, what date was it completed?**

> **How many days did it take to rebuild it?**

> **What was the reaction of the surrounding nations?**
> ○ fear   ○ loss of confidence
> ○ anger   ○ celebration

Not only had they rebuilt the wall of Jerusalem, they did it in only 52 days! The fact that this remarkable feat had been accomplished in an impossibly short time unsettled the surrounding nations and for a good reason. As verse 16 says in the NIV, "They realized that this work had been done with the help of our God."

///

GROUP DISCUSSION:
In what area of obedi-ence are you currently fatiguing? Share some biblical truths and encourage each other about finishing well in the areas you discuss.

> **What event in your life most exemplifies something that could only have been accomplished with the help of your God?**

This tiny phrase weighs a hundred pounds of inspiration. I have been so blessed by the reading and rereading of these words because it makes me think, *Have I given up believing that my life can be defined by accomplishing the supernatural with the help of God Himself? Have I been dreaming too small, chasing too little, content with what I can do with my own two hands?*

God stands to accomplish the impossible through us while too often we're content to settle for the explainable. The impossible requires taking time to listen for what He has put in our heart to do. It means believing that He will accomplish what He has spoken.

This morning I was jarred from slumber by the phone. My youngest sister Katie was calling to tell me about a meeting she and her husband, Brad, had with an adoption agency. Last year when the three of us visited the Amazon we fell in love with a baby girl who was born out of prostitution.

The baby's mother is young and, up until recently, was trapped in a relationship with a man about 30 years her senior. We found her and her child on the outskirts of a village at the tail end of a tributary somewhere in the middle of the Amazon—or as the Bible refers to it, the preciously sacred *ENDS OF THE EARTH.* Being a young mother of two, Katie was drawn to this child like a moth to a porch light. And being that the mom was abused and struggling to provide for her baby, she and Katie locked understanding like only two mothers can.

As the mom spoke in her native Portuguese to our Brazilian ministry director she pointed to Katie, "Can she take my baby?"

For those of you who know anything about overseas adoption, you know that the chances of adopting a child of a parent you've personally met is about as possible as reassembling the wall of Jerusalem in 52 days. Throw the Amazon region into the mix where most of the children have no birth certificates and you've got a situation that would require that "this task be accomplished by our God." And lest we marginalize that incredible phrase, anytime God reaches into time, space, or history to accomplish something for us, we find ourselves in the midst of a miracle. Why? Because when God helps us it is nothing short of the supernatural colliding with the natural. And this is what my family is praying for.

PERSONAL REFLECTION: Where do you need God's help right now? What have you not dreamed in His presence because you've lacked the faith or been willing to settle for the ordinary?

I'm going to have you do something a little different today by jumping ahead. Read Nehemiah 7:1-3. (We'll come back to 6:17-19.)

The wall of Jerusalem stood complete, its gates repaired and its doors hung. But this was just the beginning, as the wall was never meant to be an end in itself. Nehemiah wasted no time handpicking his own key leaders to vital roles. The first person he put in charge was his brother, Hanani. Look all the way back to Nehemiah 1:2-3 to remind yourself of his significance. The second person he appointed is Hananiah.

What reason did Nehemiah give for putting him in charge?

This description of Hananiah is a treasure I want us to ponder. It makes me wonder what his integrity and God-fearing conduct actually looked like. I wish I could see your answers to the Personal Take below, because the church is supposed to be set apart and known for its other-than-ness: Fearing God actually *looks* like something.

PERSONAL TAKE: In the personal sphere you live, what would it look like for someone to fear God more than "most people"? How would their lives be different? (Be specific.)

In addition to Hanani and Hananiah, Nehemiah appointed the Levites, singers, and gatekeepers, along with some residents to act as guards. He based all of these appointments on what we're about to read in the verses we skipped earlier. I saved these for last because this section does not follow a strict chronological order but stands somewhat alone as a description of the general time period. Go back and read 6:17-19.

What group of people are we surprised to discover were under oath to Tobiah?

This section is a little tricky, but what's important to understand is that Tobiah had at some point been a resident in Jerusalem. He and his son had even married into Jewish families. Though currently an official under Sanballat in Samaria, Tobiah had close ties to some of Judah's nobles who may have been interested in keeping an open relationship with him for the sake of commerce and trade with foreign nations. It didn't serve their cause for Nehemiah to be at odds with Tobiah, so they took every opportunity to let Nehemiah know about all the "good things" Tobiah was up to. As you can imagine, this Jewish group was a constant thorn in Nehemiah's side, as they were sympathetic to someone who blatantly stood against him. In short, Tobiah wasn't a clear enemy to everyone. We see this kind of thing play out way too often in our churches. Groups of people take sides, and leaders get hurt or altogether edged out. Instead of letters going back and forth, e-mails and texts sail through the air like arrows, parting congregations in two. Part of the rub is that sometimes the problematic person, such as Tobiah, can be someone who's known for some "good deeds" (v. 19). This can be really confusing, especially when people don't know the whole story. In Tobiah's case, whatever his good deeds were couldn't make up for his heart, which was once again revealed in verse 19.

What was the purpose of Tobiah's letters to Nehemiah?

Good deeds, whatever they may be, never trump a heart that deceives, mocks, or uses intimidation. In Jesus' day, the Pharisees did all kinds of "righteous" acts before men, but Jesus described their hearts as being far from Him (see Mark 7:6). I so appreciate the Bible's honesty that Nehemiah still had his headaches, even in the midst of a great accomplishment like finishing the wall. For the second recorded time, it was some of his own leaders who were fickle in their allegiance to him.

Personally, this kind of stuff just kills me. An enemy is one thing, but an insider-friend turned sympathetic to your nemesis because your nemesis has duped him or her with spiffy acts of kindness is insufferable!

The encouragement I can take away from Nehemiah is that he didn't appear to get all hung up in self-defense. While he did respond to the Jewish nobles' proclamations about Tobiah, he wasn't thrown off course. This is subtle but huge. May we all be careful to watch what we say, tweet, text, or post about our leaders. May we stay out of the gossip fray, petition God to reveal our motives, and not allow ourselves to be swayed merely by outward deeds.

Let us pray for our leaders, and ultimately may we rely on God for our reputations. "Remember me favorably, my God, for all that I have done for this people" (Neh 5:19).

DAY 05

IT'S ALL ABOUT PEOPLE

Funny the things you expect to happen next when reading a narrative in Scripture. When Nehemiah announced the wall had been completed in yesterday's reading, I anticipated a lively celebration would follow, one that burst forth with fireworks and a fatted calf. But nothing like this is mentioned, at least not yet. Read Nehemiah 7:4-5 and explain.

What was Jerusalem still missing?

What still needed rebuilding?

I dreamed of returning to Italy since my first visit as a high school freshman. I found the perfect opportunity after speaking at a worship conference in England. Once you cross the great divide of the Atlantic Ocean, you can jump from one European country to another like you can hop from Tennessee to Louisiana, if not beholding a tad more diversity. After all, I made it all the way to England so why not treat myself to a gelato for the price of a cheap plane ticket? After spending a few days in Florence, Sienna, and San Gimignano, I toured Venice with some friends and family to celebrate my sister Katie's 30th birthday. My other sister Megan mentioned—a few times—that she had celebrated her 30th barbecuing in my parent's backyard. This kicked off a "family discussion."

Now I'm no expert on Italy, but as utterly fairytale-ish as an entire city floating on water laced with handsome Italian men effortlessly balancing themselves on gondolas *is* … Venice was my least favorite place for one distinct reason: hardly anyone actually lives there. Because real estate is astronomically high and there's no place for cars to get around, the younger population has begun migrating outside the city, only commuting back in to work the tourism scene. According to one writer, "Already half the houses in Venice are empty, owned by foreigners and absentee landlords."[5] The sad demise of this ancient culture is heartbreaking to true Venetians because they know their city is only as majestic as the people who inhabit it.

Jerusalem was in much the same predicament, described beautifully by Warren Wiersbe. "A city is much more than walls, gates, and houses; a city is people. In the first half of this book, the people existed for the walls; but now the walls must exist for the people."[6] Up to this point not a whole lot of people lived inside Jerusalem for the walls to exist.

> **What new task did God put in Nehemiah's heart to do?**
> ○ **build a tower in the middle of the city**
> ○ **register the people who returned from exile**
> ○ **dedicate the city's gates**

We can't miss that this is the second of two mentions where God put something in Nehemiah's heart to do. The first is found in 2:12 and the second in 7:5. Look back to week 1 day 5 (pp. 28–31) and recall what God initially put in Nehemiah's heart to do.

Do you see how closely related this new task is to what God put in Nehemiah's heart the first time? Back in chapter 2 God had inspired Nehemiah to rebuild the walls of Jerusalem. Now He moved him to fill up the city with people. As mentioned before, the rebuilding of God's holy city meant nothing without God's people dwelling inside it. From the very beginning this endeavor was about more than lifeless stone and pulseless iron … it was about people. To better understand God's heart for the chosen people of Israel, read Isaiah 43:1-7.

> **In the margin list five proclamations God speaks over Israel in verse 1 and five things He promises to do for them in verses 5-7.**

The promise of Isaiah 43 carried me on its back during some of the most difficult years of my adult life. During this tumultuous time the mother of one of my closest childhood friends wrote me a letter that included the first four verses of Isaiah 43, only in place of every reference to Israel, she wrote "Kelly." I still have that precious letter.

> **What do you currently find most meaningful in Isaiah 43:1-7?**

In addition to the transcendent hope for all believers in Isaiah 43, the prophet Isaiah was prophesying that God would soon bring His people

*THE PROPHECY IN ISAIAH 43 ALSO SPEAKS TO WHEN GOD WILL ONE DAY GATHER ALL HIS CHILDREN FROM THE CORNERS OF THE EARTH SINCE IN LIGHT OF CHRIST WE ARE SPIRITUALLY SPEAKING NOW PART OF CHOSEN ISRAEL.

back to Judea from Babylonian exile.* This prophecy was fulfilled when the Jews made their way back to Israel starting about a century before what we're now witnessing in Nehemiah. A genealogical record had been made of the exiles who returned (not everyone chose to return).

As we've seen, Nehemiah had gathered the nobles, officials and common people together for the purpose of taking a census. He needed to populate the city, but he "did not want just anybody to transfer residence to Jerusalem. He was looking for Jews of verifiable Hebrew heritage. This prompted the gathering of the people for registration so each family could prove their lineage. To aid him in the process, Nehemiah found the genealogical record of those who had been the first to return."[7]

Before I have you read through the genealogy in Nehemiah 7, I want to clarify that these names were not the then-current people of Nehemiah's day but were groups who had returned from exile earlier. Still this was an important list to Nehemiah because the people moving into the city needed to be able to prove their connection to it. If this is all very confusing don't worry because the chronology of Ezra and Nehemiah is a great challenge even for scholars.

> **Turn to Nehemiah and read this record found in 7:6-60 (You can also find it in Ezra 2). Go ahead and read every name, as it will remind you that these were real people looking for their real home.**

When I read each one of these names and think of the countless ones attached to them, I consider anew the value of people. How easily I can put the ministry of people above the people themselves. The subtle temptation to exalt the "wall" of study, returning e-mails, planning events, and even putting together a meal for a Bible study over actual people is one the most counterproductive traps we can slide into. I have often found myself entirely overwhelmed with the demands of ministry, but to what end? If I've lost sight of the people for whom I spend myself, I have entirely missed the heart of why I do what I do. Besides being relevant to those in ministry, of course this pertains to motherhood, marriage, and friendship.

Nehemiah never lost sight of the purpose behind the wall: it was always for the people. This makes me think of the apostle Paul's ministry,

especially his heart for the people to whom he ministered. Read
1 Thessalonians 2:19-20, and answer the following questions.

THESSALONIANS:

> **How did Paul describe the Thessalonians? (List each description.)**

> **How did Paul refer to the Corinthians in 2 Corinthians 3:1-3?**

CORINTHIANS:

> **PERSONAL RESPONSE: If you've lost sight of people in your life
> because of the demands of the "wall," how do these Scriptures
> encourage you to refocus?**

Just as Nehemiah never exalted the walls over the people, so we must
be vigilant to see our church buildings not as ends in themselves but as
resources for the body of Christ and those who are entering the body.
The church is not a place but a people. The New Testament speaks often
to this, but I'll leave you with this one beautiful picture in particular.

> **Read Ephesians 2:19-22. Write one new perspective you have on
> the church "building" based on this passage.**

So much has happened this week in our study of Nehemiah. Most
significantly the walls were rebuilt, and now Nehemiah was readying the
people for habitation within those walls. The enemies were efficiently
handled, and the poor and oppressed were defended. The rich and
powerful repented. Leadership was established. So much has been
accomplished, but we can't forget that these milestones in Jerusalem's
progress might never have happened had Nehemiah not left the king's
resort in Persia—at least not in the way they happened. Whatever he
laid down in Persia cannot begin to compare to the joy and legacy of
being part of the restoration of Jerusalem, the joy of the whole earth. As
Christian martyr Jim Elliott so beautifully put it, "He is no fool who gives
what he cannot keep to gain that which he cannot lose."[8]

ROMAINE SALAD
WITH BLUE CHEESE, PECANS, & MAPLE VINAIGRETTE

My mom's been making this one for years. Everyone will love you for the dressing.

SERVES 6

FOR THE PECANS:
oil for the pan
1 cup pecan halves
3 tablespoons real maple syrup

DIRECTIONS: Preheat oven to 375 degrees. Lightly oil 2 baking sheets. In small bowl, combine the pecans and maple syrup and toss gently to combine. Spread pecans in single layer on one of the sheets. Roast in preheated oven, stirring once, until syrup is bubbling, about 5 minutes. Immediately scrape the pecans onto the other prepared sheet, spreading them out to cool.

VINAIGRETTE INGREDIENTS:
1 garlic clove, finely chopped
1 tablespoon fine chopped shallots
1/4 teaspoon salt
1/4 teaspoon fresh ground black pepper
2 tablespoons real maple syrup
2 teaspoons Dijon mustard
2 tablespoons red wine vinegar
6 tablespoons vegetable oil, such as corn or canola

DIRECTIONS: In small bowl, whisk together the garlic, shallots, salt, pepper, maple syrup, mustard, and vinegar. Whisking constantly, slowly add the oil in steady stream. Set aside.

SALAD INGREDIENTS:
10 cups romaine lettuce torn into small pieces (2 small heads)
3 oz. blue cheese, crumbled

DIRECTIONS: Place romaine in a large bowl, drizzle with about half of the vinaigrette and toss to combine. Add as much of the remaining vinaigrette as desired and toss again. Divide among plates, sprinkle with the cheese and the pecans, and serve immediately.

BILLIE'S
BANANA PUDDING

SERVES 8

3/4 cup sugar, divided
2 tablespoons all-purpose four
6 medium-sized ripe bananas, sliced
1/4 teaspoon salt
2 cups milk
  (whole milk works best but
  I have used skim)
4 eggs, separated
1 teaspoon vanilla extract
vanilla wafers

If you're a banana pudding fan, this one might become your new standard. Everything's from scratch except the vanilla wafers, which we may never get away from.

DIRECTIONS: Combine 1/2 cup of sugar, flour, and salt in top of double boiler; gradually stir in milk. Cook over boiling water, stirring constantly, until it thickens. Cook, uncovered, 15 minutes more, stirring occasionally. Remove from heat. Beat eggs yolks; gradually stir into hot mixture. Return to double boiler; cook 5 minutes more, stirring constantly. Remove from heat; add vanilla (this is your custard). Line bottom of a 1 1/2 quart casserole with vanilla wafers, top with sliced bananas then custard. Beat egg whites stiff gradually adding in 1/4 cup sugar. Pile on top of pudding. Put under broiler and let it brown.

Pastor Joao and Maria, Amazon village missionaries
(See their story on session 4 video.)

THE WORD RETURNS

I'VE BEEN MAKING MY OWN CHICKEN SOUP FOR A WHILE NOW, BUT I'M STILL NOT SURE I'VE LANDED THE BEST APPROACH. I KNOW EVERYONE HAS AN OPINION, BUT I WOULD LIKE THE AUTHORITATIVE, LAST WORD ON THE MATTER—THE RECIPE YOUR GREAT-GRANDMOTHER, CORDELIA WOULD HAVE GOTTEN BEHIND. I WANT TO KNOW THESE THINGS BEFORE TRAIPSING MY NEWLY PLUCKED, TICK-FED CHICKEN HOME FROM THE FARMERS' MARKET, BEFORE WASHING HIM OFF AND CHOPPING UP THE INGREDIENTS FOR A SAVORY MIREPOIX AND SHAKING IN A GUESSWORK OF SEASONINGS. IT BOTHERS ME TO THINK I COULD BE DOING THIS ALL WRONG, SPENDING THE BETTER PART OF MY DAY SIMMERING THE WHOLE CONCOCTION ONLY TO FIND I SHOULD HAVE LEFT THE LID ON. OR OFF.

The last time I made chicken soup I followed Ray's instructions from Garrett Farms who, word-for-word, told me to boil the sucker to smithereens until the meat started falling off the bones, and eat up. I tried this approach and the results were a mixed bag of tender breast meat with parts of a bird's anatomy that probably shouldn't be found in soup, ever. I assume I was supposed to, at some point, remove the carcass—though I try not to use this word when inviting people over. I'm not sure if Ray thought this went without saying, but I like to follow instructions and he didn't mention this.

Let me cut to the chase: The soup was really tasty if you didn't mind maneuvering around bones and hunks of cartilage. Personally, I thought this brought a "hearty" feel to things, but my friends felt otherwise—they're so hard to please sometimes.

Basically, I'm nearing the point of hiring someone who lives on a farm, or who's really old, to come over and tell me, "Kelly, *this* is how you make chicken stock. This. Is. How …"

I think we all long for this kind of directive at different points in our lives. We're looking for a recipe that spells out exactly how to braise the kale, potty train our toddler, invest our money, be a good mom, treat the illness. I've often approached Scripture this way: *Lord, just spell it out and I'm your girl!* Of course the Bible doesn't read this way exactly. Even in Nehemiah's day when God's commands were prevalent, the linchpin was always for His people to love Him with all their heart, soul, strength, and mind, and this you can't just check off your to-do list. At the same time, the Bible is full of crystal clear directives, principles, and commands that shed light on how we're to do life.

IN OTHER WORDS, FOR ALL THE BIBLE'S COMPLEXITIES THERE ARE COUNTLESS SPECIFICS ON HOW WE'RE TO LIVE. THIS IS NOT NECESSARILY FASHIONABLE SPIRITUALITY RIGHT NOW, AS THERE'S A PUSH TO GO STRAIGHT FOR THE ICING OF "LOVE," WHILE SETTING ASIDE THE "RULES" AS OUT-OF-TOUCH. BUT RECOGNIZING THAT GOD'S COMMANDS POUR OUT OF HIS LOVE; IT'S ESSENTIAL WE HEED THEM.

This week we'll discover God's commands (Law of Moses) to be the spiritual foundation for Nehemiah's Jerusalem. The walls were up, the doors securely hung, people were finding their way back into the city, and the surviving remnant who'd never left were renewed with the hope of a better future. Key leadership positions had been appointed. Donkeys, horses, camels, and mules peppered the landscape; while gold, silver, and priestly garments were arranged in a once ransacked temple. Jerusalem was beginning to look and feel like a real city again, but an intangible was missing—something you couldn't build with stone or buy at the marketplace. It was time for God's Word to be reintroduced to Jerusalem's society.

Without it, the people would lust and covet and act arrogantly; they'd speak meanly to one another and step over their neighbors to get ahead. They'd run after false gods and then they'd start worshiping created things instead of the Creator—just like we do today when we live apart from His voice. On the upside, if they listen—if we listen—they will see that life can be altogether different when they live according to God's commands. They'll discover that the power of God's Word that frees ourselves from ourselves is the portal to the most fulfilling experiences in the universe.

For the city of Jerusalem to be more than a bustling economy surrounded by an impressive wall, the people's hearts had to change. This could only happen if they came back to God's Word—a Word that will simultaneously make the people grieve over their depravity while quieting their weeping with tidings of grace. Without giving too much away, we'll see that the Jews needed help understanding this Word. Just like me, they needed someone older and wiser to say, "Settle down little overthinker, *this* is what that verse means. Now go make yourself a bowl of ice cream. God will be pleased." (Seriously, when you read chapter 8 you'll see I'm not too far off.)

As we enter this next phase of Nehemiah's story, my prayer is that we will be newly captivated by the truths of God's Word. Yes, the Bible is full of mysteries and grays, but there's more than enough straightforward stuff to keep us going for the rest of our lives. Though I occasionally buck this notion, I'm really happy for it because sometimes I just want God to tell me what to do—and when I look closely enough at His Word, most of the time I realize He already has.

VIDEO 4

NOTES:

_____

_____

_____

_____

_____

_____

_____

Nehemiah cared enough to lay down what was rightfully his. How did learning this cause you to think differently about what is "yours" and how you can use what God has given you for others?

Discuss the differences between giving to the poor and identifying with them.

Pastor Joao and Maria left a comfortable life in Manaus to serve the village of Puru Puru. How did their story challenge and/or encourage you?

Video sessions are available for download at *www.lifeway.com/women*

DAY 01

COMING HOME

Last week we ended with a portion of a genealogy that reminded us that rebuilding Jerusalem's walls only had meaning in so far as those walls housed people. Like twisting a pair of binoculars into focus, Nehemiah 7 sharpened a blurry wall into a sea of faces, and in the process my own vision became a little clearer. Last week when I read, "The city was large and spacious, but there were few people in it" (7:4), I had to consider what areas of my life may be cleanly laid out and finely tuned but without the end result being about people. In the margin of the next page I've given a few modern-day examples.

In the process of rebuilding the wall Nehemiah could have easily lost sight of his mission to restore the people of Jerusalem because completing a physical task can be so much easier and measurable than engaging in the often messy and less definable work of relationships.

Working with my church in the aftermath of Nashville's flood, I had days when vacuuming up drywall dust seemed much more appealing than sitting with the homeowners of that dust because the people to whom the debris belonged were suffering and you can't suck up someone's pain with a vacuum. Had our church rebuilt three women's homes while ignoring each one's pain, our efforts would have been in vain.

PERSONAL REFLECTION: Have your priorities ever gotten out of whack? Explain.

I want to anchor the rest of today's study on Nehemiah 7:6 (see p. 95), a verse you read last week. I can't imagine the trauma of being uprooted from my home and culture, forced to live in a land hostile to my beliefs and way of life. The way we celebrate, worship, cook, exercise, marry, eat, and drink our coffee, all of this differs from country to country, even region to region within a country.

My closest friends, April and Mary Katharine, decided to throw a party for all our friends and visiting family on Easter Sunday. April was born and reared in Detroit, and Mary Katharine hopped around from one deeply southern state to another, eventually landing in Nashville. I blame all their differences on the fact that Mary

Katharine likes her iced tea sweet and April finds this an abomination. When I innocently inquired about their Easter menu plans, April said she'd been planning brunchy things like french toast and mexican eggs, while Mary Katharine casually informed her that she'd already bought a turkey and the ingredients for a green bean casserole.

I know of no other way to say this except I became witness to the equivalent of a western showdown minus the guns but with that thing in a woman that will crush anything standing in the way of one of her recipes seeing the light of day on a holiday table. For a minute I thought April was going to suffer from cardiac arrest at the thought of having, what appeared to her to be, Thanksgiving on Easter morning. Then I thought, forget the heart attack, Mary Katharine is going to kill her with the knife she was planning to carve the turkey with because April was challenging her Easter menu.

I was suddenly concerned for the continuity of our at-one-time close relationships. It became apparent that April held to the belief that if you don't do brunch on Easter you are not a true American. Or Christian. Mary Katharine felt equally as strongly that if a basted turkey wasn't perched on the table, all would be lost. I could see no way of this working out because this was not just about food, this was about tradition. (We ate turkey on Easter, by the way.)

Now think about having to relinquish more than omelets and cinnamon rolls on your favorite holiday. Consider the loss of festivals and traditions passed down since God's covenant with Abraham. Think about the despair of being carried an insurmountable distance from your home, the neighborhood where your children once skipped along the streets, the temple where you met your God. Then reflect on what it would be like to try to retain your culture and heritage in a city that stood against virtually all you held dear. For us to have a deeper appreciation for what it must have been like for the Jews to finally return home, we need to further understand their experiences as captives in Babylon.

One of the Jewish exiles penned Psalm 137. Slowly read through his song, meditating on the emotions and anguish of those longing for their home. Answer the following questions.

- I made more money this year than ever before, *but* it's only benefiting me.
- My job is going better than ever, *but* I have no time for my family.
- I have a deeper relationship with the Lord, *but* I don't ever talk about it with anyone.
- We finally built our dream home, *but* most of it sits empty.

THESE ARE THE PEOPLE OF THE PROVINCE WHO WENT UP AMONG THE CAPTIVE EXILES DEPORTED BY KING NEBUCHADNEZZAR OF BABYLON. EACH OF THEM RETURNED TO JERUSALEM AND JUDAH, TO HIS OWN TOWN.
NEHEMIAH 7:6

What did the Jews do along the waters of Babylon, and why? Remember that Zion is another name for Jerusalem.

What did their captors ask them to do, and why could they not bring themselves to do it?

The Psalmist would have preferred most anything happen to him rather than forget Jerusalem, *his highest joy!* I write these words while overlooking one of the finger lakes in upstate New York where the birds are zealously chirping outside my window, as if to rouse the glassy waters. The crisp temperatures are a welcome respite from Nashville's blanketing humidity, and all is calm. But I am not home, and home is where I am most at rest. If I feel this longing for home while in a beautiful environment, I can't imagine the burn of the exiles' longing while in an unfamiliar and hostile land. This understanding makes the closing words of Nehemiah 7:6 extra meaningful: "Each of them returned to Jerusalem and Judah, to his own town." This extraordinary phrase recounts the Jews return home. So we can better understand the context for their sudden freedom to return, turn back one book and read Ezra 1:1-4.

What Persian king allowed the Jews to return to Jerusalem?

For what purpose did he allow them to return to their homes?
○ rebuild the wall   ○ rebuild their homes
○ rebuild the temple   ○ restore their farmland

Though the exiles mentioned in Ezra 2 and Nehemiah 7 returned to Jerusalem many years earlier, I'm glad we took the time to briefly look at their lives. Understanding what the Jews had been through and where they had come from give us a better grasp on who their descendents were in Jerusalem during the time of Nehemiah's reforms. It also gives us a further appreciation for why Nehemiah was so stringent about who would be chosen to repopulate the city. More on this tomorrow. ◼

I hope that the closing words of Nehemiah 7:6 were as hopeful to you as they were to me. I love the picture of each family returning to their own town. I realize, however, that not everyone studying through the Book of Nehemiah feels this hopeful. Perhaps you have lost your sense of home to divorce or betrayal. Maybe you have walked through an enormous loss in your family and the word *home* will never mean the same thing to you again. You may have lost your physical home due to financial devastation, or maybe you've had to move to another part of the country. Wherever you may be on your journey toward home, consider 2 Corinthians 5:1-5 as a balm for your soul.

PERSONAL RESPONSE: Meditate on the words of 2 Corinthians 5:1-5 in light of the truth that this world is not our true home. Journal about what part of this passage makes you long for your true, eternal home.

DAY 02
TRUE CITIZENSHIP

A quaint restaurant on the East Side has become a new culinary refuge. As my friends and I perused the seasonal courses on the menu our waiter approached us in a let-me-give-it-to-you-straight sorta way, "All my tables seated at the same time tonight so things could go a little slow." Between the atmosphere and the conversation we were in no rush. At least we knew what we were in for. With this in mind, pretend for a moment that the rest of the genealogy found in Nehemiah 7 is your meal and the following scholar is your waiter, "Chapters like [Nehemiah 7] are among the most uninviting portions of the Bible to the modern reader both because of their tedious nature and because of their overtones of racial exclusivism and pride."[1]

There you have it. *This* is what I would like to prepare you for in today's reading. Please harness your excitement. Picking up where we left off in the genealogy on week 3 day 5, read Nehemiah 7:61-73.

PERSONAL TAKE: Do you find anything troubling in these verses?

Because I often brood myself into a theological pretzel, I have a friend who regularly says to me, "Lean not Gal!" As in, " 'Lean not on your own understanding, but in all your ways acknowledge Him,' Gal!" (see Prov. 3:5-6). I'm that personality who has great difficulty leaning into the tender arms of God when I read that a whole bunch of people who willingly uprooted themselves from their homes and traveled countless miles to return to their true home had issues entering Jerusalem because they couldn't find their papers! "What form this exclusion took is unclear."[2]

Part of my unease stems from not understanding the culture and practices of the day. I can't just unlatch myself from the vigilantly tolerant and open society I live in—while experientially knowing almost nothing about ancient Jewish culture—and expect to feel right at home with today's passage. Not to mention that I'm accustomed to living in a New Testament age where there is no "Greek and Jew, circumcision and uncircumcision, barbarian, Scythian, slave and free; but Christ is all and in all" (Col 3:11). All that said, we must continue to open our understanding to the governing rules of Nehemiah's day, seeking to find a facet of the God's heart even within this troubling turn in the genealogy.

> **What three family groups couldn't prove their genealogical tie to Israel? (See Neh. 7:62.) List them in the margin.**

> **What religious group had trouble proving their citizenship (v. 63)?**
> ○ the nobles   ○ the priests   ○ the pharisees

We must ask ourselves, *Why the strict admissions policy? Why not write these folks up some social security numbers and sign some certificates of citizenship?* The answers to these questions could easily turn into their own 52-week Bible study, and some of us have laundry to do. But I want to address the profound significance of being able to prove Israelite citizenship in this era because it will give us a deeper understanding and appreciation of the New Covenant under which we now live.

First we must consider what we looked at yesterday: Virtually everything dear to the Israelite's culture, family, and religious heritage had been lost when they were carried off to Babylon. Upon their return home, it was in the Jews' interest to begin anew with as much intact from their past traditions and history as possible. Much like restoring an old home, the idea was to renew the city while simultaneously preserving its original integrity. Therefore proving their Jewish heritage was vital to all those returning. This ensured that the nation of Israel be set apart, but for a very specific end. Read Genesis 12:1-3.

> **Who would ultimately be blessed through the nation of Israel? Read Isaiah 49:3,6. To whom was Israel to be a light, and to whom would they one day bring salvation?**

I have a friend who has an enormous problem with the "exclusive" claim that Jesus is the only way to God. She finds it troubling that I would affix myself to a belief system that is so "narrow" and "closed-minded." Yet I am so drawn to Jesus because in Him there is no condemnation, favoritism, exclusivity, no running around trying to find our documents of OK-ness. The belief system of Christianity may be exclusive, but the invitation is anything but ... every nation, tribe, and tongue.

I've discovered that studying the Book of Nehemiah, specifically the rebuilding and repopulating of a city, has given me a more tangible appreciation for my own citizenship with God's people as described in the New Testament Book of Ephesians. Keep in mind that most of the believers Paul was writing to in Ephesus were converted Gentiles. They were uncircumcised, which in other words meant that they were considered the ultimate non-Jewish citizens. Read Ephesians 2:11-16.

Verse 11 says that they were "Gentiles in the _____."

List everything this excluded them from. (See v. 12.)

> REMEMBER THAT AT ONE TIME YOU WERE GENTILES IN THE FLESH—CALLED "THE UNCIRCUMCISED" BY THOSE CALLED "THE CIRCUMCISED," WHICH IS DONE IN THE FLESH BY HUMAN HANDS. EPHESIANS 2:11

Studying Nehemiah makes me appreciate even more that through Jesus' death and resurrection Jews and Gentiles can now come together as one.

Fill in the blank from Ephesians 2:14: "He is our peace, who made both groups one and tore down the dividing _____ of hostility."

PERSONAL REFLECTION: What strikes you as ironic about Jesus tearing down the *wall* of hostility between the Jews and Gentiles? Note your thoughts in the margin.

After being in Nehemiah for the past few weeks this feels like a new position my muscles aren't used to holding. After all, we've been vicariously tapping our hammers while simultaneously holding our swords for the sake of this wall, for the sake of keeping the enemies out and the Jews safely in. We've just watched good, well-intentioned people be denied admittance within those same walls to preserve Israel's purity. If Jerusalem's walls are about anything, they appear to be about division. Which brings us to the incredible irony of Ephesians 2:14 that Jesus tore down the dividing wall between the Jews and the Gentiles.

See how this comes together: Under God's direction Nehemiah and the Jews vigilantly rebuilt the walls of Jerusalem expressly for the Jews, making a way for a Jewish Messiah to one day come for the purpose of tearing down those dividing walls. Or in other terms, "God separated the Jews from the Gentiles that He might be able to save the Gentiles also. 'Salvation is of the Jews' (John 4:22)."[3]

If this is at all confusing, continue reading Ephesians 2:17-20. According to verse 19, who are we as believers in Jesus?

Perhaps the idea of groups of families and certain priests scrambling for their Jewish identification—and not being able to find them—is as unsettling to you as it is to me. Part of our unease may be due to the areas of our souls where we feel inherently disqualified. Like if someone asked us to prove our citizenship in the City of Good and Normal People With No Baggage we might be searching for our documents forever. I felt this sense of disqualification as recently as the middle of last night—the fear actually woke me up. Imagine my renewed sense of relief when part of my daily reading this morning was Ephesians 1:13-14.

PERSONAL RESPONSE: Read this passage and write what it means to you personally. Take a few minutes and rest in the peace of knowing His blood is proof of your citizenship. Let that knowledge free you from the lie that you aren't good enough in a particular area of your life.

We must learn to see today's difficult passage in Nehemiah 7 in light of the whole counsel of the Bible. To preserve the continuity of the old Jerusalem with the one being rebuilt was essential so the nation could reestablish its foundation. Though holding strictly to the genealogical records seems unbending, we can never forget that the purity of Israel was ultimately so its flame could burn without clouds of soot, shining brightly to the ends of the earth. "God had great things in store for Jerusalem, for one day His Son would walk the city streets, teach in the temple, and die outside the city walls."[4] Because of His death, Jews and Gentiles alike are now able to prove their citizenship in Christ, not through documentation that can be lost or written in error, but through His blood. Our proof of citizenship is not validated by a piece of paper but by the seal of the Holy Spirit. Someone please give me an amen.

DAY 03

THE WORD OF TRUTH

A.W. Tozer wrote that, "Truth is a glorious but hard mistress. She never consults, bargains, or compromises."[5] *Truth* can be a controversial word. We ask, "What is truth? Can it change? Does the word *absolute* ever fit before it?" We even wonder whether or not one could ever truly know it. I am well acquainted with this mind-set because I am a product of my generation, and at the same time, because I believe the Bible is God's Word, I believe truth is what sets us free.

If truth sets us free, then it certainly must exist and be knowable. Such a concept is a contentious notion to someone who doesn't believe in the Bible, but to me it is of utmost comfort and offers me great hope. Now, of course, this doesn't mean that truth hasn't been flat jarring to me at times; it has terrified me in guilty moments and redirected me when I was flying down the road in the wrong direction. But whether God's truth is acting like familiar hands gently steering me in the way I should go or tapping me on the shoulder when I'm straying—or beating my buns, it is my anchor. It is my freedom.

Because I love truth and believe we can know it, I'm excited about today's passage in Nehemiah 8, which is about truth being restored to a community. Jump in by reading Nehemiah 8:1-8. You'll want to back up to 7:73b to get the flow.

What new, prominent character has appeared?

What book did he bring out and read for the people?

In the margin list the three categories of people who listened to his words, and how long they listened (see vv. 2-3).

1.

2.

3.

*I'm trying to picture both my 2-year-old, red-headed nephew, Emmett, who all but lives to torture my 4-year-old, olive-skinned niece, Maryn, standing outside for approximately six hours quietly listening to Ezra read from the Law of Moses. Granted, I'm assuming they'd be on the young side for what this passage is speaking about, but unless Mickey was up there, this setup wouldn't have stood a chance. Yet it thrills me that men, women, and, literally translated, "**ALL WHO COULD HEAR WITH UNDERSTANDING**" were invited to listen to God's Word.[6] To think that as an awkward, often anxious little girl, God would have had a word for* **ME.**

I love this for so many reasons but mostly because it suggests that as soon as we've developed any ability whatsoever to understand, God is anxious to speak to us. We see here that God's Word isn't just for adults, any more than food and water is only for them, but that God's Word is for all of us—even for the little people.

PERSONAL TAKE: How does Deuteronomy 6:4-7 speak to this truth?

The Deuteronomy passage is a treasure to me because my parents raised my siblings and me that way. It didn't matter what the situation, my parents always drew me to God and instructed me in His ways as we went about life. They took natural (and sometimes forced) opportunities to integrate God's truth into our everyday realities, teaching us that the Bible was not a distant book far removed from our lives but was actually the light of it.

Francis Schaeffer particularly demonstrated this holistic view well. The famous pastor, author, and apologist founded L'Abri, a chalet where people from all beliefs were welcome to live, converse, and do life with him and his wife. Two women who did not share the Schaeffer's beliefs at the time (they later became Christians) recalled their relationship with the Schaeffers by saying, "Whenever [we] mentioned a good musical we had seen in Lausanne, or told about the latest French or Swedish movie, somehow the conversation always worked back to Methuselah, Moses or Mephibosheth, or to Shadrach, Meshach, and Abednego."[7] I love this, particularly because I know that Francis Schaeffer was a brilliant man who had a deep appreciation for art and culture; these were not cuckooville spiritual references but ways he could draw the truth of life back to the truth of God's Word.

This may seem obvious, but it's such a good reminder. In verse 8:1, who had given the book of the Law of Moses to Israel?

How often I forget that God's Word is a gift He has given to us for fullness of life and relationship with Him. Briefly turn to Psalm 119, read the following verses, and answer the questions that follow.

Psalm 119:89; God's Word is described in what two ways?

Psalm 119:105; What is God's Word to us?

Psalm 119:111; It's our heritage and the _____ of our hearts.

Psalm 119:114; What can we put in His Word?

After the people had settled in their homes, they wasted no time in getting God's Word back into their hearing, perhaps because of the years they had gone without it. The Lord had given His Word to them, and it was far from obsolete or impractical to their daily lives. It wasn't a word set apart for a Sabbath reading that only had application for the 45 minutes you were sitting in a pew. The people were deeply aware that they were to live every moment of their lives by God's words. They didn't have the sacred/secular divide to which we are accustomed today; they recognized that ordinary life was to be inspired and directed by the rule and reign of God.

How did the people respond when Ezra opened up God's Word?

We should sit with this long enough to be convicted. I've always lived in a home where at least one Bible was found in just about every stack of books. Scripture is available to me to the point where I may be overresourced—I have more opportunity to hear God's Word than I'm actually putting it into practice. This can foster a familiarity that robs us of our deep respect for the power and holiness of the Bible.

> **PERSONAL RESPONSE:** How does Nehemiah 8:5-6 reveal the places you are treating God's Word casually? How can you remedy this?

I love that it was the simple opening of the Word that drew such a gathering and aroused such a dynamic response of worship. Oh, the simplicity. The Israelites weren't looking to be entertained, checking their watches to see if it'd hit noon yet. They weren't critiquing the song selection, examining the children's program, or bummed that this week's drama didn't top the week before's. I am not taking a shot at any of the many wonderfully different ways we do church. I'm just wondering how many of us would show up for only the reading of the Bible. Is God's Word no longer enough?

I want you to see Derek Kidner's quote regarding this: "This day was to prove a turning-point. From now on, the Jews would be predominantly 'the people of a book.' At the dedication of Solomon's Temple there had been glory and beauty, natural and supernatural, to overwhelm the worshippers. Here the focus, apart from a wooden platform, was a scroll—or more exactly, what was written in it. Its opening brought the people to their feet."[8]

Before the exile they had worshiped in the splendor of Solomon's temple, assisted by all its inherent beauty. But now, under the cover of only the sky with but a platform for Ezra to stand on, it was the sole truth of God's Word that inspired their zealous worship of Him.

> **PERSONAL RESPONSE:** Spend the remainder of your time asking the Lord to restore in you an awe and wonder for His Word.

DAY 04
CELEBRATION

"Where would we be if God had not spoken? Where would you be if God had kept silent?"[9] Often I think about this quote because the truth of God's Word has literally changed, redefined, and redirected my life. What I believe about God and how I respond to His voice affects every dimension of how I live: how I handle my money, the way I speak about others, how I behave sexually, where I choose to spend my free time, what I watch and listen to, who I deeply befriend, and so forth. God's Word is not meant to create elitist or legalistic living but to be the breath of our lives.

I believe one of the reasons the Jews responded so dramatically to the reading of the book of the Law was because they viewed it as a Word not merely for a religious segment of their week, but for the whole of how they lived. When we understand God's Word as truth for all of life, it changes everything. To quote Francis Schaeffer, "There is no reason to believe in Christianity if it isn't true. ... I think there are many Christians—I mean, real Christians, real brothers and sisters in Christ, people I'm really fond of—who believe that certain things in the Christian faith are true, and yet, somehow or other, never relate this to *truth* ... and not just religious truth, but the truth of what is."[10] See page 106.◘

The Jewish leadership viewed God's law as so vital to the foundation of their city that they wanted to make sure everyone could understand its meaning. Read Nehemiah 8:7-8.

How did they ensure this was happening in such a large crowd?

A grocery store I frequent usually has one person on duty whose sole job is to meander through the aisles carrying a wooden pole with a big question mark on the top of it. So if you want to know where, say, the triple ginger, ginger snaps are located, just look for the roaming sign and the person carrying it will point you to aisle 7. It appears that while Ezra was reading the Law from the platform, the Levites were walking through the crowd answering questions and explaining the meaning of what was being read. This is such a critical mention because what would have been the point if, while Ezra was reading the Law, no one understood how it applied to their everyday lives?

What are your usual responses when you come across a passage of Scripture you don't understand? Do you …

○ pass over it and move on

○ let it fuel doubt and discouragement

○ ask your pastor or Bible teacher about it

○ discuss it with a friend

○ look for an explanation in a commentary

○ ask God to explain it to you

○ Google it

Continue with Nehemiah 8:9-12. According to verse 9, how did the people react to the explanation of the book of the Law, and why do you think they responded this way? Answer in the margin.

To understand the intended emotional nature of the gathering we need to know what kind of festival they were celebrating. Although we don't have enough time to do an in-depth study of the seven annual Jewish feasts, I do want us to have an idea of what was taking place at this point in our story. Read Leviticus 23:23-25.

True / False: This is the same date mentioned in Nehemiah 8:2.

How does your version of the Bible describe this day?

+

PERSONAL REFLECTION: Is there a particular area of your reality that the Word of God doesn't seem to relate to? Consider this and then ask the Lord to show you where His Word matters in this place.

The festival we're reading about in Nehemiah 8 was officially called the Feast of Trumpets, and just the name sounds celebratory. If it were the Feast of Bagpipes I could understand packing the tissues, but this was the Jewish equivalent of our New Year's Day (for modern-day Jews, Rosh Hashanah). It was a special day for God's people to begin anew and remember the grace God had poured out on their lives. However, the people were weeping instead, probably because after Ezra read God's commands aloud they realized how far short they had fallen.

How refreshing that Ezra, Nehemiah, and the Levites quickly reminded the people that this was not a day for mourning. Each verse in Nehemiah 8:9-11 mentions the sacredness (or holiness) of this day as the primary reason why the people should lose their sackcloth in exchange for their party hats. "Three times in this short paragraph it is pointed out that holiness and gloom go ill together."[11]

Does someone need to hear this today as much as I do? Though at times we certainly need to "go into the house of mourning," grieve our sin, and repent, there are also days when we should cue the trumpets, throw on the filets, and clink our glasses. I'm a melancholy at heart, so this is an inspiring passage for me to lighten it up a little. It is an extraordinary encouragement to remember that God loves celebration, community, feasting, and lightness of heart, especially when it is directly connected to Him and His grace in our lives.

This morning I had coffee with my friend April because we were meeting to pray about a trip several of my family and friends are about to take to one of our favorite places overseas. Somewhat perplexed, she kept saying, "I'm just so joyful about this trip. I have so much expectation. I've awakened every day this week so excited!"

*Then she'd say, "I wonder what all **THIS** is about." As if we had to dissect this thing called joy, like it was a foreign bug on the science table none of us had ever seen before. Like we had to explain its presence or make an excuse for it. Finally I said, "You know what? You've got joy because this is going to be a ridiculously awesome trip! Our friends will be there, our family will be there, we're going to be in a beautiful part of the world, we're going to eat well, we're going to talk about God, we're gonna laugh our heads off. Good. You've got joy. It's what you **SHOULD** have!"*

> **What explicit reason, beyond the day being sacred, does Nehemiah give for why the people should not grieve? See verse 10 in margin. "The joy of the LORD is your _____."**

I can't wait for you to see this next part. The Hebrew word for "strength" is *maoz,* and it means "refuge, stronghold, fortress, place of protection, …helmet."[12] So in essence, the joy of the LORD wasn't so much their physical might but their safe haven. The joy of the LORD offered them covering from the harsh winds of reality, and especially in their case it

NEHEMIAH SAID, "GO AND ENJOY CHOICE FOOD AND SWEET DRINKS, AND SEND SOME TO THOSE WHO HAVE NOTHING PREPARED. THIS DAY IS SACRED TO OUR LORD. DO NOT GRIEVE, FOR THE JOY OF THE LORD IS YOUR STRENGTH." NEHEMIAH 8:10, NIV gave them protection against the consequences of falling short of the Law. This was a day to remember God's magnificent grace in their lives.

PERSONAL RESPONSE: How has the joy of the LORD been your literal protection or refuge?

+

PERSONAL RESPONSE:
If you have repented of a past sin, yet it's still causing you grief and regret, write a prayer asking God to calm you in His presence.

Look back at verse 11. What did the Levites do for the people? Then what did the Levites tell them to do?

When the people were reminded of all that God had intended for them in the Law, they were overwhelmed by how greatly they had failed. As a community, it can be easy to let morality and behavior patterns slip if we look to one another to set our standards. When God's Word takes center stage and we begin to see the chasm between where we are and where we are supposed to be, some serious grieving and weeping results.

God, however, in His magnificent grace, oversaw leaders who essentially told the people, "There's a day for mourning, but today is not that day!" Their words were like a warm blanket to the Jewish souls chilled by guilt and regret. Words like *still, calm, joy, strength, choice food, sweet drink*. Sounds like grace to me.

Anadara writes: "The Enemy often turns remembrance into grief and regret; grief and regret usually stem from something done in the past. As I was studying this week I realized that if we have been forgiven, then God has also taken up our grief and regret; therefore to hang onto those emotions and give them a front row seat in our emotional life doesn't honor God and what He has done to forgive us. It also just steals our joy and freedom. The Enemy would like to remind me of my past sin, but instead I need to choose to remember what God did to forgive me and set me free!" ✚

When the grace of God gets a hold of us, we get to exchange the bagpipes for the trumpets. As the Jews tangibly celebrated God's grace with a lavish feast, celebrate today in remembrance of His forgiveness.

DAY 05

JOY

I admit that I've complicated joy. I've tangled it up with health, financial security, a nice home, entertainment, pleasures, career advances, and relationships. We could all keep the list going. "If we have a vacation on the books, we have joy. If the promotion happens, the dress fits, the boy calls, well then … *joy!* We look for little pockets of happiness to sustain us like quarters being popped into our joy meters—which are always ticking, always gobbling up whatever we just fed them." True joy is different. Unencumbered, uncomplicated joy needs nothing but the presence of Christ to light its wick in our hearts. Joy frees us from "having to constantly feed the meter with our next big plan, pleasure, or purchase."[13]

If you're like me, you may be thinking, *This is great in theory, but this doesn't play out in real life.* I get this because it was my thought process for many years as a Christian. Obtaining joy felt much like trying to catch a butterfly with a torn net—I could never quite get at it. The problem was not so much the net but that I was chasing the wrong butterfly. I ran around grasping and striving for pleasure and happiness while joy just perched there quietly on my shoulder as if to say, "Hey … I'm right here."

Discovering real joy "required some retooling of my daily routine and the way I was living my commission as a Christian. I had to start planning for joy and putting myself in its path. Like a good fisherman, I had to know where the honey holes were, where joy bit most often."[14] My hope is that by the end of our study through Nehemiah we'll discover more of the places where joy lives so our joy may be full. Read Nehemiah 8:13-18.

> **After the people went home in celebration, who stayed to study with Ezra? Priests, Levites, and _____ leaders.**
>
> **What did they discover written in the Law? (See v. 14.)**
>
>
>
> **After practicing this part of the celebration, what does verse 17 say they had?**
> ○ **great faith**   ○ **great strength**
> ○ **great joy**   ○ **great repentance**

To find out more about this specific feast, turn back and read Leviticus 23:33-44. What was the name of this Feast (see v. 34)?

How long were the Israelites to live in booths (tents)?

*So I know what you're thinking ... **WHAT DOES CAMPING FOR A WEEK IN TENTS HAVE TO DO WITH JOY?** Listen, I just got off a week-long trip where I was outdoors for seven solid days in unmentionable heat and humidity that curled my hair into next year, without product I might add. I showered in river water and lost my one and only towel on the first day. Oh, and one morning I had a sweet potato for breakfast. So I'm with you on the potentially confusing camping/joy combo. Just know this should all make more sense by today's end.*

Leviticus 23:43 sheds some light as to why everyone was to live in booths for a week. What reason is given?

Remembrance of God's work in our lives is a theme that runs throughout the Bible. Today, one of the ways we remember our deliverance from sin through Christ's death on the cross is by communion; in those days, the people remembered their deliverance from Egypt by way of feasts and special observances. Though the Israelites had regularly celebrated the Feast of Tabernacles, which was a time of harvest and celebration, they had not been observing the part about living in booths. But this was vital to their experience because it was a tangible reminder of how the Israelites had once lived when they wandered through the wilderness. When these newly returned exiles broke off branches, built shelters, and left their homes for a week to reside in simpler structures, they were reminded that God had brought their forefathers from Egypt, sustained them through the desert, and now had placed them in homes in the land He had promised.

PERSONAL TAKE: Why do you think this tangible experience of living in booths caused the Israelites to have such great joy?

I love that the Israelites celebrated this Feast as a community. Building a tent by yourself and crawling into a sleeping bag alone at night doesn't have nearly the festive ring to it as does gathering, building, and being adventuresome all together. Nehemiah 8:16 tells us that some of the people built their booths on top of their roofs while other tents peppered personal courtyards, town squares, and even the courtyard of God's house. Think of the stories this annual campout would have provided for scrapbooks for years to come! Sort of like Minter vacations gone wrong; if this had been a practice during my childhood we would still be lamenting over how our booth wasn't nearly as refined as the rest of the street's. How ours collapsed at least every other night.

Think about the little boy and little girl skipping beside their daddy with palms in their hands on their way home from the myrtle tree, "Tell me again what we're going to use these for, Daddy." Then he would tell them the story of their relatives being held captive in Egypt and how God used Moses and his staff to part the Red Sea. How the Israelites passed through on dry land, and as soon as the last Israelite toe hit the other side the Sea closed up on those menacing Egyptians and their chariots. In a more solemn tone he'd tell them about the desert wanderings, the bread from heaven, the grumbling, and the big wrong turn of the golden calf. He'd explain to them about the 40-year consequences and God's unfathomable compassion and forgiveness. He'd talk about the Jordan River and the battles they fought for the promised land. As the sun set and each family snuggled into their make-shift dwelling place, everyone in Israel would fall asleep with a little clearer picture of where they had come from and a brighter hope for where they were going; knowing that the faithful God who carried their forefathers would carry them too.

+

PERSONAL REFLECTION: What about the Christian life gives you the most joy?

One of the deepest joys of my life is worshiping, traveling, learning, and doing missions together with other believers. If you're not actively serving in community you're missing out on a joy for which there is no substitute. ✚

PERSONAL RESPONSE: How are you currently serving God and others in community? If this is a weak area, take some time to pray about a way you can get involved. Joy awaits there for you.

Earlier you looked up Leviticus 23:43 and wrote that God had told the Israelites to dwell in booths during the Feast of Tabernacles because He wanted their descendants to know about the great deliverance of the exodus. You may have also noticed that the final phrase of this verse is, "I am the LORD your God" (NIV). You see, if the Israelites had missed that the LORD was *their God*, this whole ordeal would have been little more than a religious exercise. It would have turned into a rote tradition that everyone would have tried to be out of town for—*not booth week!*

But to the newly returned exiles, reinstating this practice was a deep comfort to them as ones who had lived 70 years in captivity, wondering if God had banished them forever. To celebrate this feast in Jerusalem was nothing short of a miracle of grace, a tangible reminder that the God of Israel was still their God and evermore would be.

If you've lost your joy over God's amazing grace in your life, maybe you've lost the remembrance of your past captivity and His remarkable deliverance of you. This is not a call to revisit old, dark places but to remember your salvation. You can do this by gathering together with some friends. You can journal about the healing God has brought about in your life. You can share your testimony with someone, like Anadara did during our first nog gathering for this study. It was spontaneous, hard, and funny all at the same time—and once again we were all amazed by the way God saves. If you want, you can pitch a tent on your roof for a week, as many still do this in places like New York City. Whatever you do, celebrate God's grace with the fervor of the Israelites, "They had not celebrated like this from the days of Joshua son of Nun until that day. *And there was tremendous joy"* (Neh. 8:16, emphasis added).

CAPRI'S PASTA
WITH SUMMER TOMATO, VEGETABLE, & SAUSAGE

SERVES 6

2 squash (medium to large)

2 zucchini (medium to large)

2 pints cherry tomatoes

6 italian sausage links

1 (16 oz.) package farfalle pasta
(substitute 1 box of quinoa for a
gluten-free alternative)

4 tablespoons olive oil, divided

sea salt and freshly ground pepper to taste

parmesan for garnish

*Don't be thrown-
off by the word
"summer" in the
title cause you
will want to eat
this year-round.
It's become a
regular favorite.*

DIRECTIONS: Chop squash and zucchini into bite-size squares and place in large bowl. Cut cherry tomatoes in half for a juicier sauce, or leave whole. Toss vegetables and tomatoes in 3 tablespoons olive oil, sea salt, and freshly ground pepper.

In saucepan, pour 1 tablespoon olive oil and cook sausage. Once sausage is partially cooked, drain fat and then add the vegetables to the saucepan. Cover the sausage and vegetables and allow to cook on medium-high heat for approximately 15 minutes. While sausage and vegetables are cooking, boil water and cook pasta according to package directions. Once vegetables and sausage are cooked, remove sausage and cut each link into bite-size pieces, placing back into the saucepan once cut.

Once pasta is cooked, drain and place in large bowl. Serve pasta on individual plates and spoon sausage, vegetables, and tomatoes (and naturally occurring sauce) over pasta. Grate Parmesan cheese over each dish.

Note: You can grill the sausages, as well as the vegetables and tomatoes by placing them in a grill basket. This brings a great flavor to the meal. Sometimes I will pull everything off the grill when the sausage, vegetables, and tomatoes are almost done and transfer to the saucepan to finish cooking so their flavors can mingle. (If I grill the tomatoes I leave them whole.)

Carissa, Tim, and adopted daughter Belle
(See their adoption story on session 5 video.)

SESSION 5
A PEOPLE PRAY

WE'RE NEARING THE END, AND THIS IS PRECISELY THE POINT WHERE I START GETTING WEIRD. AFTER MONTHS OF SPENDING CONSECUTIVE HOURS IN SOLITARY, RIFLING THROUGH COMMENTARIES AND CONCORDANCES, AND INHALING COPIOUS AMOUNTS OF BURNING CANDLE WAX, ALL WITHOUT A LOT OF OUTSIDE INTERACTION, I START TO BECOME SOCIALLY AWKWARD. LIKE I'M NO LONGER SURE HOW TO HAVE A SIMPLE CONVERSATION WITH THE CASHIER AT THE GROCERY STORE BECAUSE THIS TYPE OF MEANINGLESS BANTER TAKES PRACTICE, BELIEVE IT OR NOT.

I just ordered a bunch of tacos from my favorite taco truck so I could bring home dinner to my Mexican cuisine loving friends. On the way to my car I passed by two acquaintances I hadn't seen in a while, and this caused me inordinate anxiety as a recently self-diagnosed, Nehemiah recluse. They were lost in conversation, which provided me that split second opportunity to either dash by un-noticed or push myself out of my monkish shell and say "hello," opening myself up to the now tricky task of small talk.

"Hey there Jill," I mumbled, bravely choosing interaction. She turned around, and as I bent over to tap my other friend Scott on the shoulder one of my sweet potato tacos slipped out of my bag and overturned onto his foot. He was wearing flip flops. He now had salsa and red onion on his toe. Scott is an attractive, single man, making this a much more desperate situation than all the other times you drop tacos on people. Scraping the insides of a taco off of someone's bare foot whom you haven't seen in a while—when you could have slid by with your dignity in hand—is maddening to say the least. Trying to hang onto any sense of coolness was impossible at this stage—cool had fallen out of the bag with the taco. (Scott and I share a birthday, so later when our birthdays rolled around, he sent me a little note: "We should celebrate together—quick, come throw a taco on my foot." At least he's letting me move on.)

After a few seconds of nervous conversation while balancing my remaining tacos, I hustled to my car in a heap of shame wondering what writing this study on Nehemiah had done to my social skills. I began to wonder if all the alone time, along with the tangled and confusing genealogies, had finally gotten to me. But of course I couldn't abandon Nehemiah on week five, not after all we've been through with him, not when I know he's about to pull people's beards out (Nehemiah 13 reference for you to look forward to).

Perhaps you are pushing through as well, though I can only hope with a bit more dignity. As we begin the last two weeks of our study I can't wait for you to discover the remaining five chapters, perhaps the most overlooked portion of Nehemiah. Let's face it, if you've got 45 minutes to deliver a knockout message out of Nehemiah, you're probably going to go for the whizbang how-to-complete-a-wall-in-52-days sermon, which is how most of us have known about Nehemiah. Though a remarkable part of the book, the often missed treasures and subtleties to come are some of my personal favorites. I can't wait for us to discover them together.

As you enter this week's study I encourage you to keep pondering what God has put in your heart to do, and for whom He's put in your heart to do it. If you've had trouble discerning what this might be, don't fret if you're not experiencing supernatural visions and dreams that you're hoping will make your entire existence make sense. Remember that Nehemiah's vision to rebuild the wall of Jerusalem wasn't accompanied by a flurry of signs and wonders. Quite the opposite, actually. Nehemiah heard from God based on a profound need, and I think we can all agree we're surrounded by plenty of those.

After being informed of the need, Nehemiah prayed. Again, no hallelujah choruses mentioned, just a focused season of petition as Nehemiah sought God's heart on the tragic situation in Jerusalem.

It's worth noting that so far we've read nothing of angels, burning bushes, or talking donkeys. Instead, we've seen God use what we might consider ordinary to bring about extraordinary transformation: prayer, repentance, willingness, hard work, sacrifice, humility, faith. Though miraculous displays of God's power are to be desired and cherished, I'm equally impressed with God speaking silently to Nehemiah's heart in the most "normal" of circumstances. Be encouraged that our common, everyday realities are ideal environments for God to put something in our hearts to do. According to Nehemiah, it is possible for Him to do this wherever a need appears, coupled with a willing heart to pray and to act.

DO NOT FORSAKE THE TRUTH THAT GOD HAS CHOSEN YOU, LOVES YOU, AND HAS SET YOU APART FOR WONDERFUL WORKS IN HIS KINGDOM (SEE COL 3:12).

Keep seeking Him for the "area of ministry" He has assigned to you (2 Cor 10:13). You may not encounter angels, but you might be part of a wall going up in 52 days. I'm just thrilled with either.

VIDEO 5

NOTES:

_____

_____

_____

_____

_____

_____

_____

Discuss the specific ways God's Word has changed, comforted, saved, inspired, convicted, or moved you.

Understanding that God's words to us are directly connected to our joy, describe how this encourages you to spend more time with Him and in His Word.

How is Carissa's story of adopting Belle a picture of your own adoption through Jesus? In what ways can you practically love the orphan, widow, foreigner, sufferer?

Video sessions are available for download at *www.lifeway.com/women*

DAY 01

CONFESSION

We're leaping from a week of feasting and celebration to one on confession because when you study through a book of the Bible you go where it says. Stepping out of a joyful scene and into one of reflection and lament is not how I would have laid out the study, but that's the beauty and surprise of Scripture. Part of the reason for the change of setting is because scholars differ on the date of chapter 9. The chapter begins on the 24th day of the same month but isn't explicit about which month. Some believe it's the 7th month, which naturally follows what we just studied in chapter 8, while others believe this date fits a couple months later and belongs in the time line of Ezra 10. I tend to fall with the latter, mostly because chapter 8 is largely about celebration and feasting and chapter 9 is about confession and repentance. It seems odd that the leadership would make a point to instruct the people to celebrate and not to mourn in chapter 8 and then two days later find them in sackcloth and ashes. But either way, wherever chapter 9 falls in history does not change the heartbeat. Its message to us remains powerful regardless of when it happened.

To further excite you we're about to read through the longest recorded prayer in the Old Testament, which is covered in its totality in chapter 9. This corporate prayer is a beautiful way to kickoff week 5, especially for those who need a break from the slightly more technical elements of Nehemiah. This chapter gathers some of the most notable highlights from the Israelites' history and edits them together into an easy to understand best-of reel. (Or a worst-of, if you consider the golden calf disaster and people flinging God's law behind their backs.) My point is that we're about to get to the heart of the matter, trimming back chronology and genealogical conundrums to reach the stuff of life. If you allow yourself the time and permission, this prayer will gather you in the wings of its humanity and fly you to the feet of the God of our fathers. We are sinful, weak, fickle; He is holy, strong, and faithful.

> **Though we'll spend the next three days working our way through this prayer, I want you to read it in its entirety. So settle in and read Nehemiah 9:1-35.**
>
> **PERSONAL REFLECTION: What most stands out to you?**

What two confessions did the people make in verse 2?

1.

I've been confused about the word *confession* over the years, or at least
I've gotten it jumbled up with brow-beating myself or repeating how
sorry I am. Some overlap may exist, but I want to define confession for
us, hopefully discovering some much needed freedom. First consider the
Hebrew word for confession, which is *yāda'*. It means, "to express praise,
give thanks, extol, make a public confession, make an admission."[1]

2.

Confession isn't confined to expressing sins. We can also confess God's
name, our faith, or a truth. When we confess, we are simply agreeing
with God or telling the truth about a matter. Sometimes our confession
will be about our sin, other times it will be about God's goodness,
majesty, faithfulness, compassion.

Understanding confession has helped me a great deal because it keeps
me from slinking away from God in guilt, regret, and shame; it frees
me to speak the truth before Him. *God, I confess I'm angry. I confess I'm
believing a lie about You. I confess I'm afraid. I confess I don't want to do
what You're asking me to do. I confess I'm bitter toward this person.* This gets
me on the same page with God, and once I'm on His page I can further
confess what is true about Him: *God, I know You want me to live free of
anger. You have called me to live in forgiveness. I confess that you want
me to walk in obedience,* or whatever the truth is that we need to agree
with Him on. As we study chapter 9 over the next few days, keep an eye
out for confession and the freedom and healing it brings—whether it's
confession of sin or confession of who God is and what He can do.

Before reading further into the prayer, remember that the Jews have
come out of 70 years of exile in their not-too-distant past. They have
witnessed the walls of their once powerful city lying in ruins. At the
moment, Jerusalem stands mostly empty and surrounded by enemies; it
has even been home to the rich exploiting the poor. Though Jerusalem
is on the upswing, the Jews have much to bring before the Lord as they
seek to fill the city whose walls they have just rebuilt. As they seek for
Yahweh to once again be their all in all. Go back and read verses 5-6.

PERSONAL REFLECTION: The Jews began their prayer by confessing truths about God. Pulling from these verses, what truth about God means the most to you in this season? Respond in the margin.

Now that the Jews have set the tone by confessing who God is, they begin to recount His faithfulness to them as a people. They will continue this remembrance throughout the chapter, all of which we will look at over the next three days. Remember that part of their desire to gather together, repent, and proclaim God's historic faithfulness to them stemmed from the difficult days in which they were living. Derek Kidner puts it beautifully, "The barely habitable city, the encircling heathen, and the poverty and seeming insignificance of the Jews are all transcended by the glorious reality of God. The facts are not ignored, as the ensuing prayer will show, but they will be seen in the context of eternity (*everlasting to everlasting*) and of God's unimaginable greatness (*above all blessing and praise*)."[2]

PERSONAL RESPONSE: Based on Kidner's quote, what difficult "facts" in your life can you bring before the Lord while offering them up in light of "eternity … and of God's unimaginable greatness"?

Confessing God's faithfulness doesn't mean ignoring the hard facts in our lives but reminds us that He is the only One who can truly handle them. Look back at 9:7-12.

With whom did God choose to make a covenant? (See v. 7.)
○ Moses   ○ Paul
○ Adam   ○ Abraham

Turn to Genesis 17:1-8 and read more about God's covenant with Abraham and his descendants.

PERSONAL TAKE: Based on the Jews' current difficult situation, why do you think this part of their history was important for them to recount to the Lord?

In Nehemiah 9:8 what did God find out about Abraham's heart?

It's small phrases like these that usually make me get up from wherever I'm reading and go rummage around for a pen because I cannot leave a verse like this un-underlined. It's just not right for words like these to sit all bare on the page without someone's lines, stars, circles, or boxes saying *You are special!* Which is why I have this marked in my Bible, because the statement impacts us if we allow it to penetrate our lives. *Does God see my heart as faithful toward Him?* This is a supreme desire of mine but one that can easily get confused with, *Does God see me as pretty decent compared to everyone else?* See the difference? As we wind down our time today, I can't think of a better phrase to reflect on. ✚

+
PERSONAL RESPONSE: As you consider your own life, what is threatening your faithful heart toward God? Spend some time confessing this to the Lord.

> **PERSONAL REFLECTION: Having a faithful heart toward God looked like something in Abraham's life. Read Hebrews 11:8-12,17-19. What did it look like?**

A faithful heart is not necessarily a perfect heart. Abraham had a few big seasons of sin that hurt his wife and put the lives of others in danger, yet something in his heart still rung faithful to the ears of God. I pray my heart will always beat with this kind of faithfulness and devotion even when I lose my way and stumble into sin. I believe this is only possible because of God's covenant with us, mentioned in Nehemiah 9:8, "and you made a covenant with him" (NIV). God's blessing toward Abraham can be explained not merely because of Abraham's faithful heart but also because of God's unchanging promise to him. This covenant extends to all who believe and call on the name of Jesus, as Galatians 3:7-9 says.

> **Understand that those who have faith are Abraham's sons. Now the Scripture saw in advance that God would justify the Gentiles by faith and told the good news ahead of time to Abraham, saying, All the nations will be blessed through you. So those who have faith are blessed with Abraham, who had faith.**

Our part is to be faithful; His part is to be a covenant God. It's a sacred dance no one quite understands this side of heaven, yet we are invited to dance it anyway.

DAY 02

REMEMBRANCE

Bright green and pink shoes of all little-kid sizes sprinkled the yard. Some had been repurposed into kickball bases, and some were still just sneakers making it a little confusing as to where you were supposed to run once you nailed the ball over the fence, or "killed it" as the kids yelled for me to do.

I hadn't played kickball in awhile—like 22 years—so my first kick looked devastatingly middle-aged. It secretly depressed me actually but this was no time for therapy. I sprinted to first base and was pleased with myself for making it there before being smacked in the thigh by a big rubber ball. *Safe!* I apparently still had it.

I hoped that safely making it to first base would solidify my athletic standing with my teammates, as little 7-year-old Mary Holland hustled over and gently grabbed me by the wrist. "Um, Kelly, you need to try to run more bases when you have the opportunity." Her blue teardrop shaped eyes peered up at mine like, *I'm here to help.* That sad moment in life hit me—when you realize you're not a kid anymore but a big, fat grown-up plodding from base to base in your 4th of July pants. I didn't even want sparklers after this.

Growing older may mean a little less finesse on the ball field, bigger bills, and possibly even mom-jeans, which I'm so concerned about having happen to me. But I unabashedly treasure a few gems of adulthood, and one of them is the gift of remembrance. The older we get the more history we have with the Lord, meaning we can reflect on more of His faithfulness in our lives.

If you do it right, remembrance is like compounding interest for your faith. As Christians the beauty is that our remembering shouldn't be confined only to our own lives. As we see in this collective prayer of the Jews, we're free to remember a few thousand years back, clinging to the God of the Israelites and the promises that remain for us today. As you continue to read the prayer of the people in chapter 9, let their remembrance inspire your own. Pick up where we left off yesterday, and read Nehemiah 9:9-15.

Go back through these verses and make an abbreviated list of what God had done for His people. See my examples. You'll find approximately 11 actions.

1.	7.
2. *Heard their cry*	8.
3.	9.
4.	10.
5. *Divided the sea*	11.
6.	

Yesterday's portion of this prayer focuses on who God is, while today's focuses on what He has done. See how beautifully the two go together?

> **PERSONAL REFLECTION: Write about one significant thing God has done in your life over the past year and how this is an expression of who He is.**

I love that verse 9 begins by saying God saw and God heard. Perhaps you need to be reminded today that God sees where you are and hears your cry. The wording reminds me of Genesis 29:31, "When the LORD *saw* that Leah was unloved, He *opened* her womb" (emphasis added). One of the worst things we can believe about God during a season of hardship is that we have somehow escaped His view or His hearing. He is the God who sees *(El Roi)* and the God who responds.

> **Look back at Nehemiah 9:10. What did God do in response to what He saw and heard?**

> **PERSONAL RESPONSE: If you feel a certain area of your life is invisible to God, confess this and ask Him to reveal to you the truth that He sees you. (Remember our definition of *confession*.)**

As I join in the Jews' remembrance, I am grateful for phrases like, He gave "them light on the way they were to take" (v. 12, NIV) and "spoke to them from heaven" (v. 13). Who couldn't use a little clarity on the way you're supposed to take with your marriage, job, health crisis, friendship, child-rearing? Who's not desperate to hear the voice of God speak to you with words straight from heaven? Historical proclamations like these remind me that God is not distant. He guides, speaks, and clearly lays out a way for us to live through His commands and laws.

God gave laws the NIV describes as "just and right, and … good" (v. 13). Another reminder that God's laws and commands are not to make us miserable Christians void of every pleasure outside of church potlucks. They exist so we can know life in its truest sense.

With what did God satisfy the hunger and thirst of the desert-wandering Israelites (see v. 15)?

When I read about God providing food and drink, it's easy to gloss over because I've never actually gone without food or drink a day in my life, unless by choice. I only relate to this desperate need metaphorically, like, when I'm thirsting for peace He grants it or when I'm hungering for His Word He satisfies me. In recent years I've gained a fresh appreciation for the meaning of these words as I've visited families in Africa and the Amazon who had no idea from where their next meal would come.

When I spoke to a jungle pastor about how he survives without any support, he shrugged his shoulders and turned out his palms, all with a huge smile on his face. I didn't need to wait for the English translation of his response because his countenance said it all, "I have no idea, but somehow God always provides."

May I insert my unabashed plug for taking a mission trip or even staying in your own town to visit the poor or the sick? The people you minister to will never be the same, and nor will you because the poor often give back with a faith the rest of us tend to be severely impoverished in. We give what they don't have, and they give what we don't have, and oftentimes we walk away with the far greater bounty (see 2 Cor. 8:12-14).

Continue reading Nehemiah 9:16-18. How did the Israelites tragically respond to God's faithfulness toward them?

Verse 17 says that in their rebellion they appointed a leader so they could return to their slavery. Their place of slavery was Egypt, the physical country of their bondage.

If you have the extra time, for a much fuller picture of why they desired to return, read Exodus 16–17; 32. I'll give you the short form—whenever the Israelites faced difficulty in the desert they chose to believe something false about God. Three of the biggies were that He had abandoned them, withheld from them, or wouldn't meet their needs. This in turn led them to remember their unspeakably oppressive days in Egypt through rose-colored glasses, as if their 400 years in Egypt had been one continuous ride on the "It's a Small World" boat.

The sad thing is I can relate. I have experienced times when I doubted God and subsequently wondered if the old days of my bondage were really all that bad. When I find myself here I always have to remember that two things are at play: I'm believing something negative about God in my present and believing something positive about the days of slavery from my past. Both beliefs are false.

> **PERSONAL REFLECTION:** Have you ever wanted (or are wanting) to return to your slavery? What were or are you believing about God and your past that is false?

We must never grow numb to the fact that God is "forgiving … gracious and compassionate, slow to anger and rich in faithful love. … *Even after* …" (Neh. 9:17-18, emphasis added). How I love the use of "even after" at the beginning of verse 18, because every one of us could fill in our own blank. For the Israelites, God was gracious *even after* they fashioned a golden calf and called it God! Our false gods and disobedience may look different, but I'm so grateful that because of Christ's death, His blood has covered all our *even afters*. End today by reading Nehemiah 9:19-21, and thank God for His great compassion.

DAY 03

BREAKING THE CYCLE

The length of the prayer in chapter 9 is starting to make me forget that we're still in the Book of Nehemiah. The beauty is that this walk through Israelite history shows us the background to the Book of Nehemiah while connecting it to God's unfolding plan of redemption. Romans 15:4 says everything written in the past was written to teach us so we can have hope through the endurance and encouragement of the Scripture. Chapter 9 has already done this for me, and we're only through the desert wanderings. We haven't yet hit the promised land, the prophets, or the exile, but we'll see allusions to them today as we gain a deeper appreciation for God's enduring compassion and patience with us. Allow yourself to settle into the story line as you read Nehemiah 9:22-31.

I'm sure you're noticing the cycles of God's blessing, the people's rebellion, God's loving discipline, the people's repentance, God's blessing, the people's rebellion, and so forth. The prayer maneuvers through this cycle for reasons we'll look at more closely tomorrow.

In the meantime, briefly paraphrase God's blessings and the ways Israel rejected Him in the chart below.

	God's Blessings	Israelites' Rejecting
Nehemiah 9:25-26		
Nehemiah 9:27-28a		
Nehemiah 9:28b-30		

PERSONAL REFLECTION: Out of all the different forms of pulling away from God you noted in the chart, do you relate to one more than the others? If so, explain in the margin.

PERSONAL TAKE: What do you think caused the people to respond in those ways to the Lord, especially in times of blessing?

Most of us can relate to periods of disobedience or more shocking seasons when sin wrapped its tendrils around us like an octopus clutching us from behind. We know what it's like to be straight-up defiant, lured away by lust, or deceived by subtler sins like self-righteousness, greed, gluttony. We've taken God's mercy and grace for granted, even becoming arrogant like we somehow deserve all our gifts and blessings. This is why I try not to ever let Deuteronomy 8 get too far from my thinking. I want you to read the passage for yourself. Read Deuteronomy 8:10-18.

These verses shed light on why the Israelites rebelled in times of blessing. According to the passage, for what connection between seasons of blessing and forgetting God do we need to watch out?

We may not have hopped over literal snakes and scorpions in our past, or gone without food, but most all of us have walked through seasons that felt like a vast and dreadful desert or a thirsty and waterless land. You may even be in one of those wilderness wanderings now wondering how much longer you can scrape by on manna and suck drops of water out of a rock. I pray this is a timely word for you—and not a cheer from the cheap seats—God purposes to bring you through these times so "in the end He might cause you to prosper" (v. 16).

I went through several years marked by loneliness, a singing career struggling to stay in Music City, and loss of dear friendships. I was a heap. Most days my stomach was in knots, I was crying on the phone to my mom, or both. My parents prayed a lot—you can't underestimate the power of praying parents. I write all this because God has since radically changed my life and delivered me from both the trials outside of my control and the ones I so brilliantly created myself. Now when I look around at any blessings or goodness in my life I have not a doubt as to where they came from. Though I'm never past needing to remind myself, this is rarely a fuzzy concept. This perspective came expressly as a result of those terribly painful days that proved to humble me.

> In Deuteronomy 8:10, what did the Lord tell the Israelites to do after they had eaten and were satisfied?

> PERSONAL RESPONSE: What blessing, gift, or talent are you taking credit for? Set aside a few moments. Close this book if you have to, and praise the Lord for what He has given you.

PERSONAL REFLECTION:

Turning back to Nehemiah, I am so grateful for the number of times the people confessed that God had historically acted with compassion, patience, and deliverance. I don't know what it is about our legalistic and condemning minds that sometimes don't want to embrace this glorious part of God's nature, but it is our sin not to. He is so good to us and does not treat us as "our sins deserve" (Ps. 103:10), and today's reading is a good reminder for me to confess this truth in my prayers more often.

The whole of chapter 9 has been overwhelming to write about because each verse presents a host of tributaries we could venture down for days at a time. In keeping with my clever Amazon analogies, if you've read something over the past few days that captured your attention I encourage you to paddle your canoe down its windy creek and let God speak to you. For those who need this directive in print, I'm leaving a blank Personal Reflection in the margin for you to fill in if something in this prayer has tugged at your heart. ✚

Here's one of my own reflections. Nehemiah 9:29b says, "They sinned against Your ordinances, which a person will live by if he does them." One of the ways that the word *ordinance* can be defined is God's "prescribed way."[3] Though I still struggle at times with believing or understanding that God's prescribed ways are truly best, I've become more and more convinced that this is inerrantly so. To know God's Word and to obey His ways bring us nothing other than life itself; I can think of nothing more I'd rather be than wholly alive.

DAY 04
A PLEA FOR HELP

I had been invited to take part in a three-day forum on ethics with 20 other people from different cultures, languages, and religious faiths. I anxiously accepted, totally uninfluenced by trifling side notes like where it would take place … you know, overlooking Lake Geneva in France. I remember being nervous about how my faith would stand up under people much smarter than I, with wider life experiences and broader knowledge. I also wasn't sure how I felt about liver pâté. I was surprised by the end of the weekend that my faith had actually been bolstered, especially after comparing the gods of Greek literature with the God of the Bible. Many in the room believed in a distant force, resigning themselves to a fate they could not appeal to nor appease. This seemingly hopeless faith made me newly grateful for my intimacy with Christ, a Savior I can call on when rejoicing or in need.

As we near the end of the inspiring prayer of chapter 9, I cannot tell you how thankful I am that our God is personal. He is swayed by our prayers and responds to our cries for help. We will see this truth displayed in the following text as the Jews collectively detail their difficult circumstances before their God. Read Nehemiah 9:32-37.

Though the walls had been rebuilt and God's Word was being restored to Jerusalem, describe their current crisis according to verses 36-37.

In the midst of this hardship, verse 32 tells us that the people were clinging to the truth that God keeps His …

I'm sure you noticed that in verse 32 the prayer went from being a recitation of Israel's history to a direct plea for help. Up until this point the people have recounted the cycles of God's mercy and Israel's rebellion, noting such periods as the sin of the golden calf and the days of the judges, all the way up to their more recent past of the exile. Now we find them linking all this history to the chain of their current circumstances. The mentality is that if God has acted mercifully in the past, perhaps He will do the same in the present.

I mention this because I don't want you to miss the way the Jews connected themselves to the larger story of God's covenant with Israel. No matter what period a people live in, we tend to detach ourselves from the past works of God, wondering whether He still acts as powerfully in the present as He did in the past. The people in Nehemiah's day refused to do this, clinging tightly to God's gracious covenant with them. Turn to Genesis 17:7. You'll remember this verse from day 1.

True / False: This covenant included the Jews of Nehemiah's day.

The three basic promises of God's covenant with Abraham were: (1) land, (2) kingly descendants, and (3) blessing all nations through Abraham. To put our faith in something that has not been promised us is crazy or at best vainly hopeful; to refuse believing in something God has guaranteed us is equally ludicrous. But what if we're clinging to a legitimate promise we're not witnessing in real life? The Jews knew the Abrahamic covenant was theirs for the believing. Yet when they looked around, they saw a disparity between what should have been and what actually was. Put another way, they knew that "to serve and enrich a foreign régime is [not] what was promised to Abraham and his seed."[4]

According to Nehemiah 9:36-37, what were the people supposed to be enjoying in their land?

Instead, where was it all going?

The Israelites knew they were slaves because: (1) the harvest God intended for them was going elsewhere; (2) their bodies and (3) their cattle were under someone else's control.

One of the ways we can tell we're enslaved to a false god is when the harvest God intends for us to enjoy is going someplace else. I'm not talking about godly generosity here but when we're giving our best away for the sake of securing the approval or attachment of someone. Same thing when we don't have control over our bodies but are bound to food, a person, fear, the television. As well, we know we're enslaved when we've lost control over what God intends for us to rule over, just like the Israelites' no longer could do as they pleased with their livestock. Essentially, we know we are living as slaves when we're not enjoying what God has promised to us.

The beauty is that we can find our way out of slavery by turning our hearts back to God through confession. He's a God of mercy, grace, compassion, love, patience (all attributes mentioned in this chapter). He is a God known to deliver His children "time after time," as wonderfully stated in verse 28.

For New Testament believers the news gets even more amazing. The people in Nehemiah's day were bound by the promises of the Old Covenant, but today we're under a New Covenant. Read Hebrews 9:14-15.

Who is the mediator of this New Covenant?

Now turn to Hebrews 10:19-23. According to verse 22:
We are now able to "draw _____" to God
With a sincere heart "in full _____ of faith"
Having our hearts "sprinkled clean from an _____ conscience"

Sometimes we hold the truths of Hebrews 10 hostage in the attic of our brains. We don't allow them to roam down the stairs into the chambers of our heart, across the hall into our souls, and eventually to recline in the seat of our emotions. For many of us a clear conscience and a pure heart for the purpose of drawing near to Jesus remains an intellectual understanding, sadly separated from our realities.

Just as the Jews realized a disparity when they put their slavery and oppression up against the promises of the Old Covenant so should we be able to recognize when our lives do not accurately mirror the promises of the New. We deny the love of Jesus when we cling to self-hatred and resist the offer of a pure conscience by hanging onto guilt. Too often we forsake intimacy with Christ because we're unwilling to draw near to Him. The Jews were looking to a just and faithful God; we get to look to our merciful High Priest, Jesus Christ.

PERSONAL RESPONSE: What keeps you from drawing near? Confess this to Jesus and allow Him to sprinkle your heart clean. (I often have to remind myself that guilt bears no fruit.)

Turn back to Nehemiah and read the last verse of chapter 9.

I love how this verse begins, "In view of all this …" In other words, in light of God, their past, and everything that had come upon them, the Jews were ready to make some changes. We'll read about what these changes are tomorrow, but for now keep in mind that this binding agreement with the Lord is the result of the peoples' repentance. They had confessed their sins and now were ready to live differently, reminding me of a well-known passage in James.

Read James 1:22-25 and summarize its message in the margin.

Hearing the Word of God and living differently as a result of hearing are two different things. James 1:22-25 impacted my sisters, Megan and Katie, while we were in the Amazon together. We were putting on a children's camp when a little boy fell limp, fainting right in front of us. We learned he hadn't eaten in four days. After feeding him two plates of pasta, Megan wouldn't leave his side until she got him to smile, which understandably didn't come until after she'd given him his first Starburst. The reality of starvation pummeled us. We knew full-well it existed, but we had never known it with a name and a face we could run our fingers over.

After we got home Katie tucked a picture of the boy in her Bible next to James 1:22-25 because she never wanted to forget. God had been speaking to her about materialism and selfishness, and seeing the condition of this little guy was the agent for change God used in Katie's life. She said, "I've looked into God's Word like I've looked into a mirror. I see where I need to change, and keeping this boy's picture will help me remember the change I'm committing to. I can't walk away and forget what I've seen."

PERSONAL RESPONSE: Repentance always means change. If you need to make changes in your life, write about them below. Know that, in the words of James, you will be blessed in what you do.

DAY 05

CHANGE

===

> Please read all of Nehemiah 10. Give yourself a few extra minutes to ponder the specific reforms the Jews made (you can skim over the list of names at the beginning). Ask the Lord to show you what He wants you to see.

James Montgomery Boice wrote, "Many people … do not show growth in their walks with Jesus Christ because they do not want to change the way they are living. At times they might even be moved to tears by their failures. But they do not surge ahead because basically *they want to do exactly as they have been doing*" (emphasis added).[5] I would put this more delicately except it's so perfectly the truth. So many times I've longed for my circumstances to change while *I* haven't been willing to change.

This was not the case with the Jews; the reforms they implemented proved the sincerity of their prayer. They were so intent on adjusting their lives to God's ways, they drew up a declaration of obedience that the priests, Levites, leaders, and nobles signed on behalf of the people. This passage has been a good reminder for me of the sacredness of oaths, especially in our culture where flippancy and easily broken promises are so common. It's also been a fresh challenge to make sure that my prayers of repentance are followed up by actual change because this is the hard part. It's the difference between signing your name to the credit card receipt of a new bike and actually pedaling the thing up a hill when you'd rather be eating cheesecake.

> Let's look at a few of the Jews' new commitments. What did the people promise to stop doing in Nehemiah 10:30?

Remember this was not about racial superiority but about purity toward the Lord. Non-Jews such as Ruth, Rahab, and wives of notable "heroes of the faith of Israel" were from surrounding nations and were gladly accepted.[6] The danger was that if a man or woman married someone of foreign descent who practiced false religion they would be led away from the heart of God by destructive pagan practices. Today however faith in Jesus defines the people of God rather than physical heritage. Still we need our deep ties to be with faithful believers because two people cannot be bound together while walking in opposite directions in life. My fear is that people have twisted Old Testament commandments like this (and New Testament ones like 2 Cor. 6:14) into justifications for being elitist and self-righteous or for distancing ourselves from anyone who doesn't believe, vote, worship, or act like we do. This is to miss the point of the gospel. As my professor friend, Dr. Steve Guthrie, likes to say, "We are to be set apart, not set against."

In Nehemiah 10:31 the people committed to not making any purchases on the Sabbath so they could honor it as a day of rest. This is always a good reminder for me—not that I'm a big Sunday spender, but the idea of setting this day apart is important even in New Testament times. We also read that the people planned to let the land rest every seven years.

What does Exodus 23:10-11 name as the purposes of this practice?

I love that the Lord always has the poor on His mind, often paired with the widow, alien, and fatherless in Scripture's pages. I never tire of being reminded that this is who God is.

PERSONAL TAKE: I wonder if this seventh year break was hard for the workaholic. Was it a welcome sabbatical or a year of fidgeting and loss of identity? Thoughts?

The commitment to serving and paying a temple tax is so important because it shows that the people took ownership of their place of worship along with offering support to their spiritual leaders. Though the Jews had received support for the temple from Persia at one point, Nehemiah knew this was ultimately the responsibility of the Jewish people. Whether it was giving money, contributing resources such as crops or wood, or donating their time, the Jews were involved. One of my favorite verses in Nehemiah 10 is the closing one, *"We* will not neglect the house of our God" (v. 39, emphasis added). Though we live in a New Testament age, the church has always been founded on giving, fellowship, support, worship, togetherness—in a word: *community*.

PERSONAL REFLECTION: Ponder the ways you are serving the body of Christ. Remember that your gifts, personality, and resources are desperately needed.

Though today we're unfamiliar with these reforms, each one has to do with one or more of four things. Next to each reform in the table below, write People, Work, Material Possessions, or Money based on with what each reform had to do. Note the ones I filled in for you and the reasoning behind my response. (You can use more than one word per reform.)

REFORM	PEOPLE, WORK, MATERIAL POSSESSIONS, & MONEY
Will offer the firstborn of sons	
Families will contribute wood and their firstfruits	Material Possessions (this was a sacrifice of their material possessions)
Will give money to the house of God	
Will not intermarry with surrounding nations	
Won't buy on the Sabbath	Money, Material Possessions, Work (affected how they spent money, when they bought, and the days they worked)
Will offer the firstborn of cattle	
Will forgo working the land every seventh year	

I wanted you to roughly categorize these reforms so you could see what tangible areas of the people's lives were being affected. We can easily skim over these culturally outdated practices and miss what was so important about them, what was so *hard* about them. I think about the God-inspired changes that have been the hardest for me to make, and they've always been about one of these four things. Change was hard, usually because I didn't want to surrender a relationship, a career path, money, or something I owned. If I had to choose which has always been the most difficult point of surrender for me, I can easily answer that; people have always been my biggest idol.

> **PERSONAL REFLECTION: Out of the four, to which do you cling or wrestle with the most and why?**

Making changes in our lives can be hard, but it's our refusal to change the places God is asking us to change that keeps us stuck on the dismal merry-go-round we're too afraid to jump off yet too sick to stay on. We hold on tightly only to pass by the same old stuff exactly where it was at the last time we swirled past. A friend walked into the kitchen on a particular holiday after having encountered a painful situation. She had allowed the same thing to happen to her every previous holiday for way too many years. While stacking the dishes on the counter the Holy Spirit spoke to her, *This is old.* In that second my friend knew what changes needed to be made and in obedience to God she made them, even after years of resisting. So when this holiday celebration rolled around the next year, her life in the previous 12 months had been different, hard, good, free, exhilarating, sad, and hopeful, but it hadn't been *old.* If you have the Spirit of God living in you, you can make changes in keeping with obedience—don't let anyone, especially yourself, ever take this truth away from you.

> **PERSONAL RESPONSE: You know what's coming: Where do you need to change? What steps can you take to implement this change? (Remember the Holy Spirit brings about this heart change.)**

Reading through the Jews' public confession and their commitment to do things differently has reminded me of how vital the follow-through of obedience is to our repentance. Confession followed by change makes a lovely couplet.

A recent Sunday morning reminded me of this. We had sung our two opening congregational songs, greeted one another, and settled in for corporate prayer without any need for cues. All was going as planned until someone stood up, under our pastor's blessing, and took a moment to share about a disagreement with her husband she'd experienced that morning. We all leaned in with extra fervor like we were at the movies and someone had just torn back the curtains of a window we'd not seen in before. People stopped fiddling with their bulletins.

This brave woman had been in an argument with her husband, leading to that awful feeling of having to show up at church while being madder than hornets at one another, while making sure they were showing enough of the whites of their teeth because they were going to— doggone it—have the joy of the Lord!

After sharing with self-deprecating humor and honesty, the glint in this woman's eyes and the brokenness of her voice signaled to us all that the church script as we knew it was being momentarily set aside. Honesty gave way to repentance as she stood before us and opened up about the humbling the Holy Spirit had done in her heart in the midst of that disagreement with her husband.

Everyone else who had also had a proud thought, stray word, or silent car ride to church that morning suddenly had the freedom to confess before the Lord and one another. The Spirit blew into the sanctuary like an autumn breeze, and our prideful guards and hardened fronts were carried away like crumpled leaves on His wind. Confession had made a way for us all and reminded me of how essential it is to the health of our churches, marriages, friendships, community, and worship.

As we close our week, confess before God, confess to one another, and prepare for obedience. Change awaits …

TASTY QUINOA
& BLACK BEANS

If you haven't tried quinoa yet, you can find it at most any grocery store. It's a great tasting grain that's healthy and gluten-free.
I'm using it in more and more recipes and love it.

SERVES 8

1 teaspoon vegetable oil
  (or coconut oil)
1 onion, chopped
3 cloves garlic,
  peeled and chopped
3/4 cup uncooked quinoa
1 1/2 cups vegetable
  or chicken broth
1 teaspoon ground cumin
1/4 teaspoon cayenne pepper
1 cup frozen corn
2 (15 oz.) cans black beans,
  rinsed and drained
1/2 cup chopped fresh cilantro
salt and pepper to taste

DIRECTIONS: Rinse quinoa according to package directions. Heat the oil in a saucepan over medium heat. Sauté onion and garlic until lightly browned. Mix quinoa into saucepan and cover with broth. Season with cumin, cayenne pepper, salt, and pepper. Bring mixture to a boil. Cover, reduce heat, and simmer 20 minutes. Stir frozen corn into saucepan, and continue to simmer about 5 minutes. Mix in the black beans and cilantro.

If you want, serve with chips and Lauren's Homemade Salsa (p. 139).

LAUREN'S
HOMEMADE SALSA

2 cans diced tomatoes
   (even better if you've risked your
   life by canning your own)
1 medium diced white onion
1 bunch cilantro
2 limes, juiced
3 garlic cloves, minced
1 jalapeno, chopped
   (amount depends on heat preference)
salt to taste

This is a super simple salsa recipe if you want something healthy and fresh to serve alongside Lauri's Beef Enchiladas (p. 32) or Tasty Quinoa (p. 138).

DIRECTIONS: Pour juice from tomato cans into blender. Dice onion and add to blender. Chop whole bunch of cilantro and add to blender. Pulse until ingredients are mixed. Add tomatoes, lime juice, garlic, and jalapenos. Pulse again to mix, making sure not to turn it into pulp. You want the salsa to be a little chunky. Add salt to taste. Enjoy!

Linda, founder of "The Next Door"
(See her ministry to women released from prison on session 6 video.)

SESSION 6
LOOKING FOR A NEW CITY

LAST NIGHT THE NOGS CAME OVER FOR OUR FINAL NEHEMIAH GATHERING, AND WE CELEBRATED OVER CAPRI'S SUMMER TOMATO, VEGETABLE, AND SAUSAGE PASTA DISH (SEE P. 113). I SUBSTITUTED QUINOA FOR PASTA AND THREW TOGETHER A SALAD CONSISTING OF BIBB LETTUCE, ROASTED GARLIC, PEAR AND APPLE SLICES, GRATED CARROT, GOAT CHEESE, AND TOASTED ALMOND SLIVERS DRIZZLED WITH HONEY, DRESSED WITH BALSAMIC GLAZE AND OLIVE OIL. I MADE THIS SALAD UP, THOUGH LAURI INSISTS YOU CAN'T TAKE CREDIT FOR "MAKING UP" A SALAD, SHE THINKS ALL SALADS ARE THROWN TOGETHER BY NATURE. BUT I THINK YOU CAN FLAT WRECK A SALAD IF YOU DON'T PAIR CORRECTLY. I MUST TAKE CREDIT FOR THIS.

The days of the nogs have drastically changed since our first meeting years ago in my 550-square-foot apartment, when everyone was married without children and we discussed the Bible until midnight, while eating high-calorie foods that our metabolisms could burn off by the time we got home. Now everyone's out the door by 9:30 p.m. tops, and we eat lettuce and gluten-free grains. Tonight when Anadara showed up, she was carrying some sort of baby contraption she'd borrowed either from Alli, Carrie, or Lauri. Lauri was late because her husband got caught in the studio, and she couldn't find a babysitter. Carrie had left her two boys with her husband, and Alli walked in almost in labor. Literally. This called for drastic measures: appetizers, Kelly's Made-Up Salad, dinner, and a tin can of assorted, individually-wrapped homemade cookies from a local bakery that'd just opened. If a bunch of cookies couldn't carry Alli through to labor, I was totally at a loss.

I asked each of the nogs what single element impacted them the most from the study, and I knew you'd be blessed by their answers. I'll begin with Alli because she's about to have a baby; *did I mention in her home with a midwife?* We are so in awe of her. "For me it was a confirmation that part of my calling as a follower of Christ is to love my family well in this season. I am so focused on raising my (about to be) two young kids that I find myself feeling guilty that I am not as available to other people as I was before children. But I feel like God has shown me that I am doing the work of building the wall in my own home when I strive to train my children in the way they should go, when I feed them and nurture them and even discipline them in love. This is good work, and it will only last for a season. That doesn't mean that I close my eyes to the rest of the world; it just means that I need to take this work of raising a family as a serious calling and be faithful in that."

Carrie said her number one takeaway was similar to Alli's, but here is her close second: "Being decisive and active is an important piece to the puzzle of my heart breaking. During this study I have prayed for my heart to break more than it does for the things that break God's heart, but for me it's also about taking the step to do something about it once it is broken. Satan likes to use our busy lives and our busy minds to help us forget what we're to be focusing on. I pray my mind stays focused on what the Lord has put before me to do."

Our resident baker and coffee brewer, Lauri, shared, "I like the concept of the Jews working together to accomplish something they all believed in—building the wall and restoring dignity to Jerusalem. I loved the sense of community even in adversity, and the building for tomorrow." She also signed off with, "Now leave me alone already," but I'm not sure if she meant for that to be included.

Anadara usually brings the left-of-center gem, which we all thoroughly appreciate. "The biggest take-away for me came out of chapter 6, the conspiracy against Nehemiah. When Sanballat and Geshem were trying to pull Nehemiah away from the God-given task of building the wall, Nehemiah was on to them. He didn't go into a long song and dance about why he wouldn't come. He simply explained that he couldn't leave the great work he was doing. Though Nehemiah's enemies sent him the same message four times, Nehemiah answered them with the same message back each time. He was straight-forward about it and didn't seem to suffer from the guilt or concern that they might get angry with him. He was able to see through their manipulation and repeated effort to thwart his (and God's) mission.

"WHAT REALLY AMAZES ME IS THAT WHEN THEY ATTEMPTED TO DISTRACT NEHEMIAH A FIFTH TIME WITH RUMORS AND LIES, HE DIDN'T EVEN ENGAGE OR ENTERTAIN THEIR RIDICULOUS ACCUSATIONS! I JUST LOVE THIS AND AM LEARNING TO SEE THROUGH THE ENEMIES' SCHEMES TO PULL US AWAY FROM OUR GOD GIVEN WORK."

I can't express how valuable Anadara, Lauri, Carrie, and Alli's friendship, insights, and edits have been over the years—I don't ever want to write a study without them. Their responses to the Bible's moving truths and stories are what remind me that the Word is alive. And as we begin our final week, my prayer is that you will be more convinced of this truth than ever before.

VIDEO 6

NOTES:

_____

_____

_____

_____

_____

_____

How did hearing about the Israelites' "here we are" moment (Neh. 9:36) make you think about where you are and where God desires you to be?

Galatians 5:1 says "It is for freedom that Christ has set us free" (NIV). What does this freedom look like in your life? In what areas are you struggling to live out the freedom for which He's set you free?

Linda Leathers works with women who've been set free from prison but who need freedom of soul. What about her ministry to these women inspired you the most?

Video sessions are available for download at *www.lifeway.com/women*

DAY 01

TO BE WILLING

A well-studied, 75-year-old woman once told me, "The first half of Nehemiah has profoundly impacted my life, but I can't say I know too much about the back half." This is because at first glance reading through the last three chapters means swimming through a sea of ancient names and confusing genealogies, all so you can reach the closing shore of Israel falling back into the same sins that landed them in a broken Jerusalem in the first place. Did I mention this takes place while Nehemiah is ripping people's beards out? Motivational it is not. Which is why so many of us aren't as acquainted with the latter half of Nehemiah, because the closing chapters don't lend themselves to inspiring, upbeat messages about rallying people together to save their city and rebuild their dignity like the first half does. After the book reaches its inspiring climax in chapter 6, the whole story kind of unravels, eventually halting at an abrupt knot where Nehemiah pleads with God to remember him. But as we take a deeper look this week we'll discover that there are lots of gems in these final chapters, we just have to mine a little harder to get to them.

The even-better news is that the somewhat-awkward end of Nehemiah isn't really the end. Jerusalem's story is still being written, not to mention I'm starting to fancy the way Nehemiah closes because it's so true to real life. While we're still on this earth we'll always have pinnacles as well as valleys, languid days at sea and ones that threaten to break up our boat. A story like Nehemiah, though fitful in its final pages, ultimately paved the Jerusalem road that Jesus' feet would one day walk; the story of Jesus paves the way for the day when He returns with trumpet blasts and the New Jerusalem will appear. So as we mine through these final chapters we'll gather some interesting treasures while keeping our focus on the true end of the story; the one where every tear will be wiped away in a city where the sun will not need to shine because Jesus will be the only light we need.

PERSONAL RESPONSE: As we enter our final week I wonder what God has put in your heart to do. Look back at the end of week 1 day 5 and expound on the vision God has been stirring in your heart over the course of our study. How has it evolved?

Today we study Nehemiah 11. Since many scholars believe chapter 11 picks up from Nehemiah 7:1-5,73, you may want to review these verses before beginning today's reading to remember the context. We noted earlier that the time lines of both Ezra and Nehemiah jump around quite a bit, even scholars can't agree on the sequence of events. You will recall that Nehemiah 7:4-5 describes Nehemiah's heart to populate the city and then verse 6 jumps to the beginning of a list of names who returned to Jerusalem under Zerubbabel. Thus began an almost four-chapter hiatus from the story line of repopulating the city.

• Chapter 8 dealt with the restoration of God's Law to the people.

• Chapter 9 spanned the people's prayer.

• Chapter 10 detailed the reforms the people made.

Now it appears that chapter 11 is picking back up from Nehemiah 7:73 as Nehemiah seeks to fulfill the second half of what God had put in his heart to do: repopulate the city of Jerusalem. Read Nehemiah 11:1-4.

III

GROUP DISCUSSION: Do you live in a city? If so, out of all the challenges currently facing your city, for what do you have the greatest passion? Examples could be illiteracy, disaster relief, crime, pornography, homelessness, poverty, or spiritual lostness.

Who immediately settled into Jerusalem?
○ slaves   ○ priests
○ leaders   ○ government officials

How did the people decide who would move into Jerusalem?

The leaders and the people decided that 10 percent of those living in the outlying areas of Judah were to move into the city. Note that this was not the selection of individuals but of families, so it wasn't as if a mother would be chosen to leave her family behind. The total number of volunteers may have been chosen by lot or those may have been in addition, but either way we see a willingness from the people who moved into the city while those who chose to remain outside applauded their decision. It was no doubt a difficult move for those who willingly left their surrounding villages for the culture shock of city life, that the rest of Israel praised them shows their level of sacrifice.

What new name do we see given to Jerusalem in verse 1?
○ city of David   ○ New Jerusalem
○ holy city   ○ Zion

The next 35 verses of reading make up the tricky part, but I encourage you to read through every name, if for no other reason than when you get to the end of this study you will have read the entire book. If you're extra studious you can check out 1 Chronicles 9 to see a more thorough list of these names. Before you begin reading through this genealogy keep in mind that these are not haphazard names but people used to bring about an exciting move of God upon a once barren and broken-down city now about to swell with leaders and families of notable Israelite heritage. Read through the names in Nehemiah 11:4-36.

By building up Jerusalem with God-fearing Israelite men, women, and children, the Lord was bringing His city back to its original glory.

> **How does 1 Peter 2:9-12 tell us to be similarly used within our own communities?**

> **Now turn back to Nehemiah 11, according to verses 4, 7, and 15 from what three tribes did the new inhabitants descend?**
> The Tribe of J_____
> The Tribe of B_____
> The Tribe of L_____

> **What other groups are listed in verses 10 and 19?**

Though seemingly tedious, a plan and a structure lie behind these groups of people. First the three tribes mentioned are significant because they stayed loyal to King David's heirs when his kingdom broke away to form the kingdom of Judah. Though 10 tribes were torn away to form the Northern Kingdom of Israel, God preserved a remnant for the sake of David and Jerusalem (see 1 Kings 11:32). Though pieces of other tribes also settled in Jerusalem, these three made up the core group.

Second, the priests, gatekeepers, and temple servants were strategic to the community as religious servants and leaders to help preserve God's heart as central to the city's foundation. How gracious that God did not intend for us to labor in isolation but intelligently created and gifted us with different personalities, skills, and backgrounds. Each of the names in Nehemiah 11 represents a unique individual whom the others desperately needed. Since working for the Lord in community is one of the unrivaled thrills of our existence, turn to 1 Thessalonians 2:17-19 and read about Paul's passion for his brothers and sisters in Jesus.

What three adjectives does he use to describe them in verse 19?

1.

2.

3.

Ponder two or three amazing people God has strategically brought into your life, and in the margin briefly write about what they have meant to you.

I want to close today's study by focusing on Nehemiah 11:2, "The people praised all the men who volunteered to live in Jerusalem." Oh to be willing. *Will*-ing. It's one of the hardest words of the Christian language and yet the one that holds the most reward. Just think of the sacrifice of picking up your family and moving them into the heart of a city that's just finding its legs. Think of how many leaders and commoners would have preferred the countryside of Judah to the bustling city of Jerusalem, to wake up to roosters as opposed to street merchants and taxi cabs. You may love city life as I do, but it's not everyone's cup of caffeine. Either way, all these settlers did it for the greater joy of participating in a restored Jerusalem and the privilege of dwelling in God's chosen city. I imagine that their sacrifice is not worthy to be compared to the eternal joy of *this* being their heritage.

PERSONAL REFLECTION: Where is the Lord asking for your willingness? What changes are you afraid of? What do you fear giving up?

We may not always feel like it. We may arrive weary, afraid, or discouraged. Warren Wiersbe said it best, "Never underestimate the importance of simply being physically present in the place where God wants you."[1] Sometimes obedience simply means showing up.

DAY 02

FULL CIRCLE

If I were to tell you that the first 26 verses of Nehemiah chapter 12 included the last list of names you would see for the entire study would you be inspired to read it? What if I offered chocolate as part of the incentive? *Cheesecake?*

I know I am running out of grace here, but if you will indulge me by reading through these names I can assure you the day's study will only get better from here. Keep in mind that even scholar Derek Kidner shares our sentiments, "Unexciting as the first half of the chapter is, it has a point to make by its refusal to treat bygone generations as of no further interest."[2] As unexciting as unexciting is, go ahead and quickly read Nehemiah 12:1-26.

Two waterfalls now reside in the footprints of the Twin Towers that crumbled on September 11, 2001. A wall inscribed with 2,983 names of men, women, and children outlines each print. These lost their lives on one of the gravest days in our nation's history. Though once a harrowing war zone, the grounds are now a sacred and calming sanctuary for those who desire to honor the lives we lost. Simultaneously the setting provides a place of grief and mourning as well as a memorial of hope for the future, reminding us that we have rebuilt and are still rebuilding.

Since New York City represents one of the flagship emblems of our country, the attacks of 9/11 struck a blow to us all. When the city that inspired Broadway musicals, helped throw pizza onto the national stage, and gave us lyrics like "Start spreading the news," experienced such a day, no wonder we all felt like some stripes and stars had been ripped from our hearts.

As New York City is an American icon, to the Jews of Nehemiah's day Jerusalem was not just a symbol of their culture, heritage and race—it was the very place where God chose to dwell among His people. Even the most patriotic among us will have trouble grasping the sacred relationship between the Jews and their city, because God's presence is no longer attached to a particular city, rather He lives in men's hearts. For the Jews, the holy city now stands on the verge of renewed splendor, but before we can raise our voices and make our toasts at the dedication of the walls, we should first spend a few minutes in remembrance.

In the margin match the events below with the corresponding dates. If necessary for answers review the time line on page 13.

A. Cyrus allowed the Jews to return to Jerusalem.
B. Some of the Jews returned under Zerubbabel and rebuilt the Temple. Some of the people rejoiced and others grieved because it wasn't the splendor of the original (Ezra 3:12).
C. Nebuchadnezzar the king of Babylon destroyed the temple in Jerusalem.
D. Nehemiah and the Jews rebuilt the wall and dedicated the city.
E. Ezra returned and restored Temple worship in Jerusalem.

Now that we've taken time to stop and remember some of the defining moments in Jerusalem's history, slowly take in verses 27-43.

If tickets were available for each of the following aspects of the dedication of the wall, and you could only purchase one, for what would it be and why? Check your response and explain below.

○ the purification of the people, gates, and wall (v. 30)
○ the procession of choirs and leaders Ezra led on the wall to the right (vv. 31-37)
○ the procession of choirs and leaders Nehemiah followed on the wall to the left (vv. 38-39)
○ the choir singing in the house of God (vv. 40-42)
○ the sacrifices of celebration and rejoicing (v. 43)

During they royal wedding of Prince William and Princess Kate my sister Katie rounded the corner of her living room where my niece was kneeling in front of the television while the minister pronounced the blessing on the couple: "Mom, *shhhhh*, we're praying." At 4 years old Maryn was immersed in the royal wedding like a sugar cube in English breakfast tea. She was made for events like these: the royal processionals, the funny looking cars, exotic hats, and of course she was enamored by the train of Kate's wedding dress that flowed like a river of milk down the aisle of the royal palace.

For those who had never attended a royal wedding, an inauguration, or any notable celebration, I can't imagine that much before or since

In the right margin (time line):
600 b.c.
587 b.c. —
539 b.c.
—
538 - 515 b.c.
—
458 b.c. —
444 b.c. —
400 b.c.

could have rivaled this defining moment in Jerusalem's history. The Jews' allegiance to God was wrapped in their allegiance to the nation; they could not tear the fibers of their city away from the fabric of their faith. All was bound up together. Though in the beginning of the book all seemed lost when Nehemiah's brother informed him of the devastation, today the people could formally celebrate God's enduring faithfulness to their city and to the remnant of Israel.

Scripture does not explicitly state the starting point of the two processions, but based on other landmarks scholars believe both groups began their march from the Valley Gate. Look back at Nehemiah 2:13.

At what gate did Nehemiah begin his initial inspection?

Singing Levites and priests with trumpets now danced on a wall that once lay in ruins. The gates Nebuchadnezzar set ablaze, smoldering as the Jews were carried off to Babylon, now stood guard as choirs and leaders—as Ezra and Nehemiah themselves—passed over their newly secured and sacred bars. The very gates and landmarks we read about today are the same ones we read about in Nehemiah 2–4, only now they have been restored and reclaimed. "Every inch of these ramparts had its special memory for one group or another."[3]

At the beginning of our story Nehemiah set out from the Valley Gate in the middle of the night, all alone with nothing but a vision in his heart. Nehemiah's finely manicured hands that once served wine in a king's palace had certainly become cracked and calloused as he swept them alongside the toppled stones of what was left of Jerusalem's walls. Perhaps he stumbled over the rubble, maybe even maneuvering through the grave sites of those slain during the attacks so many years before.

+

PERSONAL REFLECTION: What do you long to see God bring full circle in your life? Write it down even if you've given up hope or think it impossible.

Now we find him standing with choirs, priests, leaders, and a city full of rejoicing citizens at a gate whose doors, bolts, and bars have now been secured. God had brought Nehemiah full circle, beginning at one broken gate on the circumference all the way around to the very same gate, only on this day all had been made new. ✚

Ephesians 3:20 says, "To Him who is able to do above and beyond all that we ask or think according to the power that works in us." What we have the hardest time asking for or imagining isn't always the scientifically-defying miracles or supernatural wonders but the common, everyday, close-to-home struggles we've long stopped hoping could ever change or heal. The splintered relationships, cold marriage, wayfaring children, unruly addictions, in these places we need immeasurably more than all we could ask or imagine.

If God began Nehemiah's journey at the broken Valley Gate and completed it at a restored one, we have reason to hope He will work with the same restorative power in our lives. He can take us from a place on life's earth where the ground is icy and the air pierces our lungs to the very same footprints—however much time later—where baby shoots of grass bend beneath our tread and the fragrance of spring quickens our senses. Where the place we stand remains the same but everything around us has changed, this is full circle. This is a miracle. Now to Him who is able to do immeasurably more …

DAY 03

TRUSTWORTHY

If you were hoping to sell a staggering number of copies of *Nehemiah: The Book* you would have ended the story back in chapter 6 after the inspiring accomplishment of rebuilding the wall. Or right where we left off yesterday in chapter 12 at the lavish royal dedication of the restored city. The author could have slapped a period on the thing at either of those points, before the Israelites had a chance to start messing things up again. But this story is clearly not about book sales or ending on a climactic note. This historical account tells us of real life: the miraculous, the mundane, the never-ending battle of staying the course of obedience. We can take so much away from this account, far more than a version that tied itself up with a ribbon at the end. Let's quickly finish up chapter 12 by reading verses 44-47. Then after a couple of questions we'll move on to chapter 13.

The priests, Levites, singers, and gatekeepers ministered according to the commands of what former leaders? (See vv. 45-46.)

PERSONAL TAKE: Why do you think these famous names are important references, given that Jerusalem is in the rebuilding stages?

Nehemiah wisely took advantage of the camaraderie and high spirits of the celebration by appointing men to make sure the storerooms were filled to support the priests and Levites. When people can see the excitement that surrounds a project it's much easier to get them involved, so it was good that Nehemiah established this in the moment and didn't let any time pass for the momentum to ebb and the enthusiasm to wane. Read Nehemiah 13:1-3.

We will look more thoroughly at this highly sensitive idea of foreigners being excluded from the assembly tomorrow, but note a couple things now. First, the reference is Deuteronomy 23:3-5 if you want to study it further. Second, other portions of Scripture indicate that if a foreigner wanted to convert to faith in the God of Israel, he or she would be welcomed. Remember that when Ruth the Moabitess married Boaz, the distinguished leaders wished her to be like Rachel and Leah who were the sacred matriarchs of Israel. So we have to take today's reading in context of the greater whole. Continue reading Nehemiah 13:4-14. You may want to top off your coffee because things start to derail a bit here.

Where was Nehemiah when these abuses took place? (See v. 6.)

Remember that Tobiah was an enemy who managed to gain allies within Judah, had a Jewish name, and had a son who had married into a Jewish family. He was a splinter under Nehemiah's skin that Nehemiah could never quite dig all the way out, even all these years later.

What sin had Eliashib the priest and Tobiah committed? (We aren't sure if this is the same priest mentioned in chapter 3.)

How does this directly defy what we just read about in 12:44-47?

In the verse appearing in the margin underline each item Eliashib stored in the room.

What was Eliashib supposed to have done with those items?

[ELIASHIB] HAD PREPARED A LARGE ROOM FOR HIM WHERE THEY HAD PREVIOUSLY STORED THE GRAIN OFFERINGS, THE FRANKINCENSE, THE ARTICLES, AND THE TENTHS OF GRAIN, NEW WINE, AND OIL PRESCRIBED FOR THE LEVITES, SINGERS, AND GATEKEEPERS, ALONG WITH THE CONTRIBUTIONS FOR THE PRIESTS.
NEHEMIAH 13:5

The Levites depended on the tithes of the people as they historically had no land of their own, and since this support had stopped being given, despite the Jews' promises to do so in chapter 10, many of the Levites had returned to places outside of the city where they could sustain themselves. The sacred storeroom in the temple which traditionally provided for the Levites, priests, and temple sacrifices had been cleared out by Eliashib to make room for Tobiah to store his household goods, his 52-inch flatscreen, mini fridge, and fraying college-boy couch with the stuffing creeping out of the seams. I am so grossed out! Today's equivalent would be a church leader blatantly stealing from the congregation's tithes or more subtly by using his God-given position for the pursuit of power, fame, or wealth. The message here for all of us is that the ministry and house of God are sacred territories not to be challenged by our lust for glory or our prideful ambitions. We don't have to commit fraud to be guilty of competing with the Lord's renown, especially when it comes to the ministries in which we serve.

Are we using any piece of the Lord's work for our own advantage, glory, or fame? Have we set aside a portion of His house as a room for our own agendas or successes?

> **PERSONAL RESPONSE:** Ask God to show you if any part of your service to Him has become about you. Let Him clean out that "storeroom" where you're housing your pride, selfishness, or personal ambition. Confess it to Him and then allow that space to be used for His renown and for building others up.

According to Nehemiah 13:8-12, what measures did Nehemiah take to remedy the problem? List all of them in the margin.

Who did Nehemiah appoint to oversee this work (see v. 13)?
- ○ trustworthy men
- ○ men with military background
- ○ wealthy men
- ○ government officials

The world doesn't need more wealth, strength, power, or skill as much as it desperately needs trustworthy people. My heart is never more at rest, my soul never more at peace than when I am in the presence of a person of integrity. I find relational serenity in never having to second-guess

FUN FACT: NEHEMIAH IS UNIQUE BECAUSE IT'S WRITTEN MOSTLY IN THE FIRST-PERSON. SCHOLARS CALL THESE PORTIONS "THE NEHEMIAH MEMOIR."

what the person really meant, not having to dodge gossip or duck drama. When I have the assurance that a person's word is true, motives pure, and intents just, I have found a rare treasure indeed. Nehemiah knew that if he was going to entrust the storehouses of the Lord's temple to anyone, it simply had to be to the trustworthy.

My dad and I were talking about this while driving in the car when he brought up a convenient car-themed, spiritual illustration. He was talking about faithful friends and ministry partners when he gestured toward my rearview mirror. "Kelly, you'll meet certain people in life who will be so trustworthy, so full of integrity you'll never have to worry about looking in that mirror to see what's going on behind you." We started naming all the people we've known and loved through the years—the people with no ulterior agendas, people you could trust with your life, those you were utterly at peace with.

I realize that for most of us, the names we just read through don't carry a lot of meaning, but they represent faithful and loyal people Nehemiah could count on. Our world could be no more in need of such trustworthy souls today. ✚

> **PERSONAL RESPONSE:** If the Holy Spirit is bringing to mind areas where you have not been trustworthy, take time to confess this to the Lord. And to a person if you need to.

+

PERSONAL REFLECTION: What gets in the way of you being trustworthy? What challenges your desire to be a trustworthy person?

Being trustworthy is a paramount quality because if a person is trustworthy, even their offenses or mistakes can be taken in this light. But if a person cannot be trusted, how can you put your hope in even their most elaborate gift? The family I grew up in wasn't perfect, but my parents and siblings have always been people I could implicitly trust, and this makes any shortcomings or offenses completely endurable.

May we seek to be people that God and others can trust, people whose deeds do not change whether we are in the dark or the light, whether we've been entrusted with little or much (see Luke 16:10).

DAY 04
NEHEMIAH'S JERUSALEM

Our work is never done: There will always be another round of laundry to fold, another season of tomatoes to peel, core, shove in a jar, and boil the daylights out of. We'll always need another haircut, until the day when most of our hair is gone and then we will have other problems. It seems that just as we've rid ourselves of that one, gripping sin we find another monstrous idol snarling in our hearts, and we're be back to that mortifying-the-flesh thing again. We achieve peace in our relationships but it's never long before someone's feelings get hurt, before *mine* get hurt. The wall gets built and the gates get restored, but it only takes a few months for a guy to trash the temple with all his "stuff."

If I sound like a big fat downer on the final pages of this study it's only because I'm what my dad likes to call a "realist," and because this is pretty much how Nehemiah ends. I promise we won't end with my melancholy propensities, not even with the final dot that's been placed at the end of Nehemiah. As I said before, Nehemiah 13:31 is not where Jerusalem's story ends, and we will end at the true end. And it will be good. No laundry will await us there. Read Nehemiah 13:15-22.

What big problem here contrasts with Nehemiah 10:31?

If you grew up in the church and were exposed to the King James language, the scenario we just read about is what we would call classic "backsliding." After the summer camp high of Jerusalem's repentance, where everyone made promises to not neglect the house of God, they had slipped back into their old ways. I can't help but quote H.G.M. Williamson here, "Spiritual growth is generally better gauged by the quality of what passes as normal than by the fleeting moments of particular uplift."[4] In other words, nothing's wrong with the spiritual highs we experience on the mountain peeks, but the way we live our daily lives down here at sea level reveals the most about us.

How did Nehemiah correct the problem in 13:21-22?

I have a lot of admiration for Nehemiah, and a smidgen of healthy jealousy, because when confronted with an issue he always had a decisive reaction. I don't mean to package him too neatly as I'm sure some days he wrestled with what to do. But we don't see a lot of wavering with this guy. He always acted decisively. Anytime I can see a matter this clearly, I consider it a true gift from the Lord. ✛

Continue reading the final verses, Nehemiah 13:23-31. What new problem has come to Nehemiah's attention?

+

PERSONAL REFLECTION: Where do you lack clarity in a particular situation? In keeping with Nehemiah's example of prayerfulness, spend some time seeking counsel from the Lord. Pray in belief!

Again, we must face the politically incorrect prohibition of foreign relationships, this time marriages. Though difficult for us to reach outside of our New Testament mind-set, inspired by a gospel that embraces all cultures and races, we must attempt to understand the context here.

What was the primary reason why Nehemiah didn't want the men to give their children in marriage to foreigners (v. 26)?

PERSONAL TAKE: Why do you think Nehemiah used King Solomon as the flagship example of someone led astray by foreign women? (See 1 Kings 3:10-14.)

On the scale below, mark the intensity of Nehemiah's reaction to the people's sin.

ANNOYED	BUGGED	MAD	SUPER ANGRY	RIPPING OUT PEOPLE'S BEARDS

This is such a feminine study. Dainty and sensitive. Bordering on delicate, really. OK, whatever … so in this quite violent moment I cast my eyes across the page and longingly gaze on the Book of Esther, happy to see a woman's name, ready to thrust myself into her arms. (I encourage you to go through Beth Moore's Bible study *Esther* if this is you too.) But if we allow ourselves to dwell on the reasons behind Nehemiah's rage, we may discover it is more an expression of love and justice than anything else.

What was the problem Nehemiah 13:24 cited about the children born to these mixed marriages?

I am so moved by the reality that children were at the center of Nehemiah's strong reaction. He saw little kids running around who couldn't speak the language that carried the message of God's truth, love, and grace for them. When he heard them speak in the tongues that would lead them to the empty arms of false gods, he literally started pulling people's hair out! When it comes to the immeasurable treasure of our children we can only hope they will be defended by the kind of passionate heart behind such actions. Nehemiah knew that "A single generation's compromise could undo the work of centuries," and he couldn't leave this up for grabs.[5]

Though totally foreign to our current way of life, we have to remember that, for the children of Nehemiah's day, Hebrew was essential to understand God and His ways. The language of Judah was the language the priest and leaders—the parents—spoke to their children about the God of their forefathers. To lose this language was in essence to lose God's Word, ultimately losing God Himself. As Williamson says: "For a religion in which Scripture plays a central part, grasp of language is vital. … When religion and national culture are also integrally related, as they were for Judaism at this time, a knowledge of the community's language was indispensable."[6]

Quickly turn to Luke 17:1-2. What does Jesus say about those who cause children to sin?

Marrying the people of Ashdod, Ammon, or Moab was a direct affront to the God of Abraham, Isaac, and Jacob. These cultures represented the false gods and beliefs that would tear God's beloved people away from Himself. Outrage was a reasonable reaction as the very lives of parents and children hung in the balance. Though clearly laws and customs have dramatically changed since these times, something resides here for us all. How grieved are we by the lies and immorality hurled at our children through the television screen? How angered are we by the rise of all manner of child abuse? How saddened are we at the moral compromises within the church?

PERSONAL RESPONSE: Have you grown comfortable with what should grieve you? Why or why not?

We have much to mourn over and much to defend, but we can only do so out of a heart that can break. Combating these enemies with legalism will not do; fighting with spears of self-righteousness is totally ineffective; condemning with harsh judgment is harmful, nor is it of Christ's character. We must have hearts that have broken over our own sin. Only then can we be trusted with confronting for the sake of righteousness and to defend God's beloved people. This takes us back to the very beginning of the book where Nehemiah wept, mourned, prayed, and fasted for Jerusalem. When it comes to standing steadfastly for righteousness we too must begin here.

DAY 05

A HEAVENLY JERUSALEM

My whole family lives in a 10-mile radius of each other, including in-laws and grandkids. I'm the only one who took off to pursue such a sound and stable endeavor as a career in music. Bless me. I love where I live, but life would be better if I could scoop up my entire family in a great big fish net, leverage them over a state, then turn the net upside down and shake them out around me. I miss so many family gatherings by living in Nashville, or "Mashmill" as my 4-year-old niece meticulously pronounces it. When my sister Katie explained to Maryn that Aunt Kelly was mommy's sister, Maryn squinted her eyes, threw back her head and said, "Mommy, you're *hilarious!*" In other words, Aunt Kelly from Mashmill is the fun friend everyone sees on holidays, but *sister?* Don't be ridiculous.

Last year when I walked in the door for Christmas, Maryn proudly introduced me to my own father: "Aunt Kelly, this is Pop Pop; Pop Pop, this is my Aunt Kelly." At 3 years old, Maryn had no reference for the fact that I have known Pop Pop longer than 10 times her lifespan, and I refer to him as Dad. She doesn't yet understand that my brother David whom she calls Uncle, my sister Megan whom she calls Auntie (they're into simplicity around there), her mom Katie, and I are all children of Grammy and Pop Pop. Generations don't mean anything to Maryn yet, and the finer points of how we're all connected don't make a lot of sense to her right now either; just make sure you come bearing gifts to her birthday party.

The way Maryn has an intimate, but very finite, perspective on our family is, I'm afraid, much how I have tended to view Old Testament Jerusalem, the Jews, and the city walls in Nehemiah. I understood them to be people and places that offered us practical lessons and motivational truths, but in my mind they were like à la carte items on the Scripture menu. Until spending significant time in Nehemiah I didn't grasp how deeply connected we are to ancient Jerusalem and her people. I knew this intellectually to a certain extent, but the truth hadn't morphed into a deeply meaningful sentiment.

Without the restoration of God's Word to the Jews' society, without the impenetrable walls, without the sturdy gates, without a restored temple, without a place for God's very name to dwell, without Nehemiah preserving the next generation by protecting their understanding of the language, where would we all be? I'm certain God would have made a way, but if you take away such a "simple" response, we are left to consider our indebtedness to Nehemiah, his people, and their work.

Not only should we consider the strings that tether us to our ancient past, Scripture also compels us to look forward to an altogether New Jerusalem. The story God was writing when He put it in Nehemiah's heart to rebuild Jerusalem's walls is a story He continues to write. This New City is a place we can approach according to Hebrews 12:18-24. The privilege means so much more to me after studying the Old Jerusalem with its strict adherence to the law and its stringent separation from non-Jews.

Read Hebrews 12:18-24 in your own version of the Bible and then read it from The Message version below.

Unlike your ancestors, you didn't come to Mount Sinai—all that volcanic blaze and earthshaking rumble—to hear God speak. The earsplitting words and soul-shaking message terrified them and they begged him to stop. When they heard the words—"If an animal touches the Mountain, it's as good as dead"—they were afraid to move. Even Moses was terrified. No, that's not your experience at all. You've come to Mount Zion, the city where the living God resides. The invisible Jerusalem is populated by throngs of festive angels and Christian citizens. It is the city where God is Judge, with judgments that make us just. You've come to Jesus, who presents us with a new covenant, a fresh charter from God. He is the Mediator of this covenant. The murder of Jesus, unlike Abel's—a homicide that cried out for vengeance—became a proclamation of grace.

The author of Hebrews is referring to Exodus 19 when God descended on Mount Sinai and spoke to Moses and the Israelites. This was no cozy, community get-together, rather it was one where God landed on the summit in flames, striking any person or animal dead who so much as grazed the foot of the mountain. He came to give the Ten Commandments and declare His people as set apart, but the glory of His presence was harrowing. Hebrews 12 reminds us that we no longer have to approach God under such terrifying circumstances but because of Jesus we now come to another mountain under a covering of grace.

What mountain do we now get to approach (v. 22)?

Name all those present in the heavenly Jerusalem (vv. 22-24).

Who is our Mediator there?
○ Moses   ○ Jesus
○ Abraham   ○ the Holy Spirit

So we can really feel the difference between the Old City and the New, I want you to see the heavenly Jerusalem detailed in Hebrews up against the earthly one described in Nehemiah.

Look up the following verses in Nehemiah and contrast them with the corresponding verses from Hebrews I've provided for you:

"You have come to Mount Zion, to the city of the living God (the heavenly Jerusalem)" (Heb. 12:22) with Nehemiah 2:17

"To myriads of angels in festive gathering, to the assembly of the firstborn whose names have been written in heaven" (Heb. 12:22-23) with Nehemiah 7:4

"To the spirits of righteous people made perfect" (Heb. 12:23) *with* Nehemiah 1:6-7

"To Jesus (mediator of a new covenant)" (Heb. 12:24) *with* Nehemiah 9:7-8

+

PERSONAL REFLECTION: How are you tangibly looking forward to this heavenly city? In what ways do you appreciate it more deeply after studying Nehemiah?

These contrasts make me long for the New Jerusalem as I appreciate how many of these New Covenant blessings can be grasped right now! We are no longer under the Old Covenant. We can approach the city of the living God boldly because of the blood of Jesus which covers us in His righteousness. Turn a couple chapters back to Hebrews 11:8-10.

According to verse 10, describe the city Abraham was looking for.

My dad has been preaching for nearly 40 years, and if I had to name his most often quoted verse (outside of Genesis 3:15—you can look that one up for fun and be intrigued), Hebrews 11:10 is the one. I inherited his restlessness so I'm with him in his longing for a real city whose very builder and designer is the One, true God. Can you imagine? After enduring the highs and lows of Nehemiah's toiling on the wall, his desperate prayers for Jerusalem, glorious praises, and angry outbursts, I am lifted by the thought that one day we will live in a whole place—a whole *city!* One that bears the same name as the one we've been studying these past six weeks. It all just means so much more to me now. ✚

Perhaps this is my clumsy effort at avoiding a drawn-out good-bye to Nehemiah and to all of you who are now my American *manas* (the Portuguese word for *dear sister).* But instead of packing up our story I'd like us to continue to cast our gaze forward because, as I've said before, our story will not end until we reach the New Jerusalem. Even then, it will be but the beginning.

As your final activity in this study, look up Hebrews 13:14 and write it out in the space below.

My Manas, praise God that the earth which is now groaning for redemption is not the city He leaves us to build our dreams upon. Praise Him that we can approach an everlasting city, the heavenly Jerusalem by virtue of Jesus Christ who presents us before God as pure and blameless. Let us never lose sight of the reality that heaven is a real place, and all that God has put in our hearts to do for His kingdom here on earth will one day translate into that New City. I implore you to take your place on the wall—whatever the sacrifice—for every stone we lay in His kingdom will never topple and the gates we secure cannot be burned. It will be a city where all disgrace will be removed both from creation and from our inmost being. Until that day, as Nehemiah so eloquently stated, "Remember us with favor, O our God" (see Neh. 13:31).

Because of Jesus, we are assured He will.

KRISTIN'S
SWEDISH GRANOLA

6 cups regular oats (not quick oats)
1/3 cup wheat germ
1/2 cup sunflower seeds
1 cup almonds, slivered
1/2 cup whole almonds
1/4 cup brown sugar
1/2 teaspoon salt
1/2 cup raw chip coconut
1/2 cup honey
1/3 cup water
1/2 cup oil
2 teaspoons vanilla

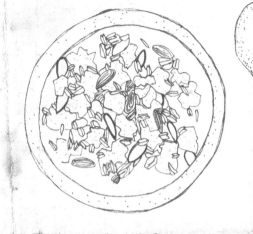

Since some of you get together in the morning, here is a fabulous granola recipe you can serve over Greek yogurt. Top with honey and fresh berries if desired.

DIRECTIONS: Combine first 8 ingredients in a bowl (through chip coconut). Combine honey, water, oil, and vanilla in a separate small bowl and stir into dry ingredients, adding more honey if needed. Grease 2 9x13-inch pans. Bake approximately 1 hour between 325–350 degrees, stirring every 15 minutes! (Watch closely at end.) Cool completely and store in an airtight container.

VIDEO 7

NOTES:

_____

_____

_____

_____

_____

_____

_____

_____

_____

How has studying the Book of Nehemiah given you a deeper appreciation for the New Testament references of Jerusalem? How has your appreciation for Jerusalem grown or changed as a result of this study?

What about the New Jerusalem are you most looking forward to? (Be specific and practical in your answer). Have you thought much about the New Jerusalem being an actual city?

Nehemiah was obedient in fulfilling what God had put in his heart to do. How has the unfolding story of his legacy inspired you to pursue what God has put in your heart to do?

Video sessions are available for download at *www.lifeway.com/women*

LEADER GUIDE

Nehemiah: A Heart That Can Break is a video and discussion-based Bible study. The weekly homework along with the teaching videos and relational interviews will promote honest conversation as you study Scripture together. Since conversation is essential to the experience, I've written a few starter questions, both in the Listening Guide and Leader's Guide, to help get the discussion rolling each week. Note that these questions are in addition to the Group Discussion questions that appear frequently throughout the study.

Your group may not need these catalysts, but if ever you hit a lull, they can be referenced. As your group gets more comfortable sharing, you may need these questions less. My ultimate hope is that each group will share its own Scriptures, experiences, and reactions to the videos, which will naturally feed the conversation each week. The added recipes encourage groups to eat together because so many great friendships and conversations naturally start around a dinner table.

Digging deep into your own life and sharing with your group will help you grow in relationship. I've always been encouraged when one of the "nogs" (Alli, Lauri, Carrie, and Anadara) has been brave enough to share something personal—it makes me feel not as alone in my own struggles and questions. Also note that different ages, backgrounds, stages of life, and races will only make your conversation and experience all the richer, so don't be afraid to share based on differences you perceive in your group.

If you can eat together and keep your group small, genuine sharing and times of prayer will be more natural. Many, however, have used *The Living Room Series* studies in large groups. We've heard of people meeting at coffee shops, swim practice, parks, large churches, and small churches, so use *Nehemiah* however fits your group.

You don't have to get a specific leader for *Nehemiah*; however, you may want to have one woman view the videos and discussion questions in advance each week and prepare materials. Sharing the cooking and hosting responsibilities is always a good idea as well, unless one person is up for the task each week. If you need any further help, feel free to visit *www.lifeway.com/women* or *www.kellyminter.com*.

SESSION 1

1. For your first session, please plan a get acquainted time. Allow each woman to introduce and share some basic information about herself.
2. View the first video and discuss the questions on the viewer guide and your hopes for the group.
3. Encourage everyone to do their study during the week and pray for the group members.

SESSION 2

1. What drew you to studying the Book of Nehemiah? What's one thing you hope to receive from the Lord over the next six weeks?
2. What was the most impacting moment for you this week? (It may be a Bible verse, principle, prayer experience, revelation, new understanding, conviction, or other.)
3. Nehemiah's heart broke for the suffering in Jerusalem while living in a Persian resort. How did discovering this impact your own heart for the poor, suffering, sick, or a family member?
4. How did the study on prayer this week cause you to think differently about prayer and/or encourage you to persist in prayer? In what ways is prayer difficult for you?
5. Nehemiah was very afraid when approaching the king to request to help his fellow Jews (see 2:2). Talk about a time when obedience meant doing something that made you afraid.
6. Nehemiah 2:12 says that God put the desire to rebuild Jerusalem in Nehemiah's heart. What do you believe God is stirring in your heart to do for someone?
7. If you have relationships with the people in your group, take a few minutes to express what gifts and passions you see in one another. Sometimes we can't see the strengths that others see in us.

SESSION 3

1. What's one of the greatest areas of need you see in your church or community? How were you challenged or helped by the way Nehemiah assessed the needs in Jerusalem?
2. What are you "rebuilding" in your life right now? What makes rebuilding sometimes more difficult than building?
3. In what practical ways can you help remove the disgrace from people's lives by being a minister of reconciliation? (See 2 Cor. 5:17-21.)
4. Nehemiah took time to pray and plan. Are you the type of person who likes to dive in and get going, or do you take time to ponder and pray over your ministry plans and desires? Discuss.
5. What unforgettable memories do you have of serving God with other people?
6. How has working side by side next to people of different ages, cultures, and backgrounds both challenged and built up your faith?
7. If you feel free enough to be open with your group, ask for prayer regarding the specific rubble in your life that is weighing you down.

SESSION 4

1. This week we learned some of Nehemiah's most difficult obstacles came from the inside. Without disparaging anyone, how have wounds inflicted on you from the inside been the most hurtful?
2. As you looked at Nehemiah confronting those who were oppressing the poor, how has your heart for justice been stirred?
3. What "rights" have you been hanging onto? How did seeing Nehemiah lay down some of his wealth and privileges for the sake of the people convict you?
4. On page 73 Anadara said that fear and insecurity can get in the way of her building her "wall." Discuss how you relate to her.
5. Nehemiah's enemies came at him and the Jews with fear and lies. How do you actively combat these two attacks that can threaten us on a daily basis?

6. When you read that the wall had been completed in 52 days, what were your thoughts and emotions? How did the truth that God had helped them accomplish this task encourage you to seek His supernatural help in your own life? (See Neh. 6:15-16.)
7. We learned in day 5 that the walls needed people. Do you find that you easily lose sight of the people in your life for all the lists, tasks, and busyness you're trying to manage? How can you change this?

SESSION 5

1. You're a little past the halfway mark: What's impacting you the most so far?
2. How did looking at the returning exiles this week make you thankful for your citizenship in Christ? (See Eph. 2:11-16.)
3. Ask someone to read Psalm 137 and reflect on what it must have been like for the exiles living in Babylon.
4. In chapter 8 the Levites made God's Word clear to the people and helped them understand it. Discuss practical ways you can be active in explaining God's truths and His heart to your children, neighbors, and co-workers.
5. God's Word moved the people to tears and also to celebration (see Neh. 8). Talk about the last time God's Word powerfully moved you either to sadness or joy.
6. Where is God's Word missing in our society? How can you lovingly, humbly restore it to the areas of your community where God has given you entrance and influence?
7. What gets in the way of your joy? What promotes joy in your life? If you can, spend some time praying for one another's joy.

SESSION 6

1. You read through the longest recorded prayer in the Old Testament this week (see Neh. 9). What was your favorite verse or passage in this prayer?
2. "When we confess, we are simply agreeing with God or telling the truth about a matter." How did this phrase on page 119 impact the way you think about confessing to the Lord?

3. Nehemiah 9:9 says that God heard and saw the Israelites' suffering. How do these two truths encourage you right now?

4. Ask someone to read Deuteronomy 8:12-14. Discuss how you can you purposefully remember God in your prosperity and abundance.

5. When the Jews saw how far they had drifted from God's Law they made specific changes in their lives. Keeping in mind that God's commands are always for our highest good, what practical changes do you need to make?

6. The Israelites pleaded with God for help at the end of chapter 9. Is there something you need to petition God for? If so, spend time with your group praying for this specific need.

7. On page 133 we read, "So many times I've longed for my circumstances to change while *I* haven't been willing to change." Do you look for change to come from everywhere else except from within yourself?

SESSION 7

1. Nehemiah 11:1-3 describes the people who willingly moved into Jerusalem. What gets in the way of your being willing before the Lord?

2. What part of the dedication of the wall did you love the most? Did reading about this glorious day of celebration and dedication motivate you to persevere on whatever "wall" you're working on?

3. What's the single-most important blessing you will take away from the your study of the Book of Nehemiah?

4. Share a story about God bringing you full-circle.

5. Describe the characteristics of a trustworthy person in your life.

6. In what ways are you personally thankful for Nehemiah's obedience and sacrifice in coming to Jerusalem?

7. How does living in the hope of a New Jerusalem change the way you are living your life on earth?

ENDNOTES

WEEK 1

1. H.G.M. Williamson, *Word Biblical Commentary*, vol. 16, *Ezra Nehemiah* (Nashville, TN: Thomas Nelson, 1985), 167.
2. Many attribute this quote to Oswald Chambers.
3. Edward W. Goodrick and John R. Kohlenberger III, *The Strongest NIV Exhaustive Concordance* (Grand Rapids, MI: Zondervan, 1999), 1407.
4. *HCSB Study Bible* (Nashville, TN: Holman Bible Publishers, 2010), 776.
5. David Kidner, *Tyndale Old Testament Commentaries*, vol. 12, *Ezra and Nehemiah* (Downers Grove, IL: InterVarsity Press, 1979), 88.

WEEK 2

1. Kidner, *Tyndale Old Testament Commentaries*, 89.
2. Mervin Breneman, *The New American Commentary*, vol. 10, *Ezra, Nehemiah, Esther* (Nashville, TN: Broadman & Holman Publishers, 1993), 182–84.
3. Ibid., 189.
4. Angie Smith, *I Will Carry You* (Nashville, TN: B&H Publishing Group, 2010), 158.
5. Williamson, *Word Biblical Commentary*, 212.
6. Breneman, *The New American Commentary*, 193.
7. Williamson, *Word Biblical Commentary*, 226.

WEEK 3

1. Goodrick and Kohlenberger, *Strongest NIV Exhaustive Concordance*, 1553.
2. Ibid., 1409.
3. Williamson, *Word Biblical Commentary*, 395.
4. Kidner, *Tyndale Old Testament Commentaries*, 107.
5. Ed Emery, "Reclaiming the Veneto," *Le Monde diplomatique* [online], April 2011 [cited 14 November 2011]. Available from the Internet: *http://mondediplo.com/2011/04/16venice*
6. Warren Wiersbe, *The Bible Exposition Commentary: History* (Colorado Springs, CO: Cook Communications Ministries, 2003), 666.
7. Knutte Larson and Kathy Dahlen, *Holman Old Testament Commentary*, vol. 9, *Ezra, Nehemiah, Esther* (Nashville, TN: Holman Reference, 2005), 208.
8. Randy Alcorn, *The Law of Rewards* (Carol Stream, IL: Tyndale, 2003), 25.

WEEK 4

1. Williamson, *Word Biblical Commentary*, 38–39.
2. Larson and Dahlen, *Holman Old Testament Commentary*, 22.
3. Warren Wiersbe, *The Bible Exposition Commentary: New Testament Volume 2* (Colorado Springs, CO: Cook Communications Ministries, 2001), 23.
4. Wiersbe, *Bible Exposition Commentary: History*, 666.
5. Allan Zullo, *Wise Guys* (Naperville, IL: Sourcebooks, Inc., 2005), 307.

ENDNOTES

WEEK 4 continued

6. Kidner, *Tyndale Old Testament Commentaries,* 114.
7. Colin Duriez, *Francis Schaeffer: An Authentic Life* (Wheaton, IL: Crossway Books, 2008), 119.
8. Kidner, *Tyndale Old Testament Commentaries,* 115–16.
9. Larson and Dahlen, *Holman Old Testament Commentary,* 215.
10. Duriez, *Francis Schaeffer,* 106.
11. Kidner, *Tyndale Old Testament Commentaries,* 117.
12. Goodrick and Kohlenberger, *Strongest NIV Exhaustive Concordance,* 1442.
13. Kelly Minter, *The Fitting Room* (Colorado Springs, CO: David C. Cook, 2011), 186.
14. Ibid., 188.

WEEK 5

1. Goodrick and Kohlenberger, *Strongest NIV Exhaustive Concordance,* 1413.
2. Kidner, *Tyndale Old Testament Commentaries,* 121.
3. Goodrick and Kohlenberger, *Strongest NIV Exhaustive Concordance,* 1448.
4. Kidner, *Tyndale Old Testament Commentaries,* 124.
5. James Montgomery Boice, *Nehemiah: An Expositional Commentary* (Grand Rapids, MI: Baker Books, 2005), 106.
6. Williamson, *Word Biblical Commentary,* 130.

WEEK 6

1. Wiersbe, *Bible Exposition Commentary: History,* 689.
2. Kidner, *Tyndale Old Testament Commentaries,* 133.
3. Ibid., 139.
4. Williamson, *Word Biblical Commentary,* 389.
5. Kidner, *Tyndale Old Testament Commentaries,* 144.
6. Williamson, *Word Biblical Commentary,* 397.

THE GREATER STORY
OF THE NEW JERUSALEM

To see the Book of Nehemiah as a story only about Jerusalem's ancient walls is to miss its much grander story of redemption. This remarkable narrative goes far beyond the personal ventures of Nehemiah and the Jews. If we don't grasp this we miss the most miraculous part of the story: the city Nehemiah rebuilt became the foundation for where Jesus Christ would one day walk. The stones Nehemiah laid, the gates he secured, and the streets that the newly-returned Jews trod, would one day be the city our Savior would weep over on His journey to the cross. The city where He would give His life for our sins.

The idea of being a sinner in need of a Savior can seem antiquated and offensive, especially in our culture. But acknowledging our lostness before God is surprisingly liberating, as it offers an explanation for the extreme brokenness we so often feel with God, one another, and even creation. Thankfully, this acknowledgment gives us far more than an explanation; it opens our hearts to a Savior. In addition, because broken sinners are His treasure suddenly we find ourselves in a surprisingly hopeful place. "For the Son of Man [Jesus] came to seek and to save the lost" (Luke 19:10).

Perhaps you have fared better than me, but I have made a terrible savior for myself. When I have turned to other gods such as people, possessions, career, entertainment, and pleasure, I have been miserably disappointed. The truth that I cannot save myself—that no other than God can satisfy—frees me, because it forms the entry point to experiencing the grace of Jesus. I just can't think of anything more awful than being my own god.

Salvation does not depend on our moral goodness, one of the primary distinctions that sets Christianity apart from other religions. We can do nothing to earn our way to God; instead God came to us through Christ. During Nehemiah's day, under the Old Covenant, the Jews had to prove their citizenship in God's holy city through their documented heritage. Now our belonging in God's kingdom comes through faith in Jesus Christ because salvation is for "everyone who believes: first for the Jew, then for the Gentile" (Rom. 1:17, NIV).

Jesus extends this beautiful offer to us at an infinite cost. He died on a cross, separated from God, so He could absorb the punishment that should have been ours. Someone had to bear the extreme destruction of our sin. Instead of us bearing it in endless separation from our Creator, the perfect Son of God stepped into our world and bore it for us. After He died for our sin, He was raised from the dead so we could be "saved by His life" (Rom. 5:10). We are not left to earn or prove our place in God's family, instead we have been adopted into His family through Jesus.

Wherever you are in the Book of Nehemiah, my prayer is that you will not only witness Old Testament Jews successfully rebuilding their city, but that you'll discover what their endeavor means for your own life. Nehemiah's broken heart to rebuild Jerusalem set the stage for our Savior to come and redeem us.

A Savior infinitely greater than Nehemiah has seen you, sought you, given His very life for you, and invited you to His table. My hope is that you will revel in the forgiveness and grace Jesus offers and you will receive the invitation of eternal life, which is to know Him, "the only true God" (John 17:3). Then you will truly understand what the Book of Nehemiah is all about.

If you have further thoughts or questions, contact us at *info@kellyminter.com*.

LISA HARPER ANGELA THOMAS MANDISA **KELLY MINTER** **JENNIFER ROTHSCHILD** & MORE

BECAUSE WE'VE BEEN GIVEN SO MUCH

A **SPECIAL EVENT** EXPERIENCE OF **FELLOWSHIP**, THE **WORD**, **WORSHIP** & **MISSIONS**

GROUP PRICING WITH RESERVED SEATING NOW AVAILABLE

SPEAKERS AND WORSHIP LEADERS VARY PER EVENT LOCATION

lifeway.com/abundance   800.254.2022

Events subject to change without notice. Sales tax applied to event cost, if applicable.

THE LIVING ROOM SERIES

RUTH
loss love
& legacy
kelly minter

...uth: Loss,
...ove & Legacy
(... sessions)

...th's journey of unbearable loss, redeeming love, and divine legacy comes alive in
... second study in the Living Room Series. If you've ever felt devastated, struggled
... a stranger, longed to be loved, or wept along the way, you'll find a loyal sister in
...th. This study includes recipes and a leader guide, plus bonus videos at
...way.com/livingroomseries

...hance your experience with *Loss, Love & Legacy*—a CD of original songs written
...d performed by Kelly to accompany this Bible study. This companion piece spans
...e realm of human experiences with contemplative and inspiring lyrics, engaging
...e listener on her own spiritual journey.

| ...ember Book | 005189427 | **$12.95** |
| ...usic CD | 005275025 | **$12.99** |

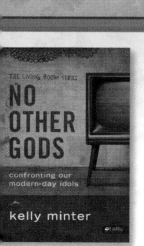

No Other Gods: Confronting Our Modern-Day Idols
(8 sessions)

The first in the Living Room Series, this thought-
provoking study encourages women to make room
for God by dethroning the functional gods that clutter
and claim their lives. A relational approach to Bible
study that includes recipes, music playlists, and more.

Member Book   005035500   **$12.95**

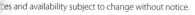